LETTERS
FROM A
SK·EPTIC

LETTERS
FROM A
SKEPTIC

DR. GREGORY A. BOYD
AND EDWARD K. BOYD

Chariot Victor Publishing
A Division of Cook Communications

Chariot Victor Publishing
A division of Cook Communications, Colorado Springs, Colorado 80918
Cook Communications, Paris, Ontario
Kingsway Communications, Eastbourne, England

Scripture quotations in this book are from *The Holy Bible, New International Version*®. © 1973, 1978, 1984 by International Bible Society. Used by permission of Zondervan Publishing House. All rights reserved.

Copyediting: Afton Rorvik

Cover Design: Joe DeLeon

Library of Congress Cataloging-in-Publication Data

Boyd, Gregory A., 1955 –
  Letters from a skeptic / Gregory A. Boyd and Edward K. Boyd.
    p. cm.
  ISBN 1-56476-244-0
  1. Apologetics. 2. Boyd, Gregory A., 1955 – Correspondence.
  3. Boyd, Edward K. – Correspondence. I. Boyd, Edward K.
  II. Title.
BT110.B638 1994
239 – dc20   93-33314
                                                              CIP

---

13 14 15 16 printing/year 02 01 00

CONTENTS

PART III: QUESTIONS ABOUT THE BIBLE

PART IV: QUESTIONS ABOUT CHRISTIAN LIFE AND DOCTRINE

Edward K. Boyd resides in Lake Placid, Florida. He is the father of 6, grandfather of 15, and great-grandfather of 9. He worked 35 years in sales management with Uniroyal Tire Company. After years of agnosticism, Mr. Boyd became a Christian at the age of 73.

Gregory A. Boyd is a professor of theology at Bethel College in St. Paul, Minnesota. He received his B.A. in philosophy from the University of Minnesota, his M.Div. from Yale Divinity School, and his Ph.D. from Princeton Theological Seminary. He is an ordained minister and the preaching pastor at Woodland Hills Church in St. Paul, Minnesota. He has authored three books and numerous articles on theological subjects. He is married to Shelley Boyd and has three children.

DEDICATION

In loving memory of Arlyle Boyd

PREFACE

Exceptionally intelligent, intensely skeptical, very strong-willed, and 70 years old—could a more *unlikely* candidate for conversion be found than my father? He had given me little grounds for hope. My father never showed any openness to the Gospel. He harbored only resentment toward the church and was outspoken in his animosity toward what he called "born-again types." The few talks about the faith he and I had had during the 14 years I had been a Christian up to the time our correspondence began had all been somewhat awkward, very short, and totally futile. I had, quite frankly, all but totally given up hope for his salvation.

Nevertheless, beginning in March of 1989 I felt strongly led of the Lord to attempt one more time to share the Christian faith with my father, this time not in a face-to-face manner but through the mail. I had in mind a long-term dialogue in which all of our cards would be laid on the table. I would give him the opportunity to raise all his objections to the truth of Christianity, and he would give me the opportunity to answer these objections as well as give positive grounds for holding to the Christian faith. To be honest, I initially thought little would come of this. But what did I have to lose?

To my surprise, my father accepted my invitation. Almost three years and 30 letters after our correspondence began, Edward K. Boyd made Jesus the Lord and Savior of his life on January 15, 1992.

For several reasons I feel it would be valuable to make this written correspondence public. First, there are multitudes of Christians who, like me, have loved ones who are not believers. Some of these loved ones are perhaps as rationalistic, as skeptical, and as apparently "hopeless" as my father was. It is my prayer that this correspondence between my father and me can be useful not only as a source of hope, but also as a resource of information for believers in similar situations. The questions and objections my father raised are the questions and objections nonbelievers most frequently have concerning Christianity.

9

Secondly, this dialogue can be helpful to believers wrestling with the rational foundation of their faith as well as for nonbelievers who, like my father, are considering the truth of Christianity. While our correspondence doesn't come close to providing anything like an exhaustive critique and defense of the Christian faith, my father's keen questions touch almost all the relevant objections and invoke almost all the relevant considerations in defense of the Christian faith.

Finally, this correspondence can be of service, I believe, to students of apologetics and personal evangelism. Far too often we view the study of apologetics as an "ivory tower" discipline with little relevance to what really goes on in spreading the Gospel. Objections to the Christian faith, we frequently assume, are "really" moral, not intellectual, in nature. What sinners need is preaching, not reasons.

It is my hope that this dialogue begins to dispel this myth. There is, of course, always a spiritual dimension in an unbeliever's resistance to the Gospel (2 Cor. 4:4), and reasons are never in and of themselves enough to convert an unbelieving heart. Prayer and spiritual warfare are also always necessary. But this by no means implies that the rational obstacles to the faith that unbelievers have are disingenuous and that believers have no responsibility for knowing and sharing the rational foundation of the faith they hold. Scripture assumes such a responsibility (1 Peter 3:15).

This correspondence is an illustration of how the intellectual and spiritual elements of an unbeliever's resistance to the Gospel can go hand in hand, and how a person can address both of these elements simultaneously. It is an illustration of how practical and effective apologetics can be. It is an example of how God can use intellectual considerations to reach and change the heart of one whose mind and heart had previously been impervious to the light of the Gospel. And, finally, this correspondence is a testimony to the transforming power of persistent love and honest communication in sharing the Gospel.

One further word should perhaps be said about this correspondence. My father and I, in conjunction with the publishers of this work, have sought to preserve the original correspondence between us as much as possible. A certain amount of editorial work was necessary for the purposes of clarity and organization (i.e., the original correspondence did not flow as thematically as it does in its present form), but we have kept as much of the original wording as possible. In most instances, for example, we did not seek to "clean up" my father's language as we felt that the omission of this would have weakened the authenticity of our dialogue. We apologize if some readers find this offensive. Similarly, in the interest of authenticity, we retained the rather informal way I sometimes quoted Scripture. Where exact scriptural quotations are intended, they are from the *New International Version.*

I would like to express my thanks to the many who have helped bring this written correspondence into book form. I deeply appreciate the students in my 1992 interim apologetics class at Bethel College for their insightful comments and editorial suggestions concerning this collection of letters. It was a pleasure to share with them the joy of my father's conversion during this course. My thanks also go out to members of my previous apologetics classes, both at Bethel and at the Church of the Open Door, for the insights they shared with me as they read various letters from my father while our courses were in process.

A profound gratitude must of course be expressed to my father for being open to this dialogue and for pouring so much of his thought, feelings, time, and life into this correspondence. His honesty, genuineness, and "no baloney" attitude shine through in a most refreshing way throughout our correspondence, and I thank him for this. I must also thank him for giving me permission from the start to share his letters with my students, and now for allowing me to share our entire dialogue with you.

And finally, my father and I both must express our utmost gratitude to our Lord Jesus Christ. As is evidenced in both of our lives, His grace truly is amazing. Our prayer is that this collection of letters will be of some use in bringing others — some perhaps previously thought to be hopeless — into this same "amazing grace."

Dr. Gregory A. Boyd

The Invitation: To Dad, with Hope

March 10, 1989

Dear Dad:

I trust all is going well with you and Jeanne down there in sunny Florida. Aside from a little flu-bug hanging around our house, we are weathering the final — very prolonged — stages of the Minnesota winter pretty well. But will spring ever come?

Here's something that might interest you. Yesterday I was invited by the Islamic Center of Minnesota to publically debate a very well-known Islamic scholar on the subject of the Trinity at the University of Minnesota. Perhaps against my better judgment, I agreed. This man is a professional debator whose academic credentials are almost encyclopedic! I'm a bit intimidated, but also excited, about this opportunity. It will occur April 13th.

This (sort of) leads me to the main point of my letter. As you know, I teach apologetics here at Bethel. Apologetics is the study of defending the Christian faith against objections which non-Christians have and of presenting positive reasons for the truthfulness of the Christian faith. As academic matters go, it is my first love. My debate with the Muslim scholar in April will be an exercise in apologetics.

What you don't know, because I've never told you, is that I have you to thank for getting me into this field. I want to thank you for this. When I first became a Christian some 14 years ago, you were legitimately concerned that I had gotten myself involved in some sort of mindless cult. (It turns out you weren't very far from wrong at the time!) So you continually challenged my faith with questions and objections. I didn't much appreciate it at the time, but I certainly do now, and I love you for it. You forced me to think seriously and critically, about what I believed and why I believed it. You got me into apologetics.

After about a year, however, our discussions about Christianity came to a halt. Your concern lessened, I think, as my Christianity became more mature and less "cultic" and narrow-minded. On several occasions since then I have raised up the issue of Christianity in a general sort of way with you, but we've never really pursued the matter in much depth. And this brings me to the point of this present letter.

Dad, I would really love to enter into an in-depth dialogue with you about why I have continued to be a Christian for the last 14 years. This isn't only, or even primarily, because I love apologetics. It is mainly because I love you. No one can blame another person for wanting to share something which is most valuable to them with another person whom they love, and that is what I'd like to do with you. My faith in Jesus Christ, my experience of His saving power and love, is the single most precious thing in the world to me — and I really believe it is the most precious thing any human being on this earth can have. I also believe that a relationship with Christ is the most important thing a person can have since it has, in my view, eternal consequences.

It struck me as odd and wrong that I spend so much time discussing Christianity with others when I have not discussed it in-depth with my own father, whose care and concern got me into this field in the first place! You're 70 years old now, and frankly, I think it's about time that I begin this discussion. It also just seems right, as a part of our father/son relationship, that we be open with one another about our worldviews.

Now I know you, Dad, so I know that my "preaching at you" would do absolutely no good. (I tried that the first year I was a Christian, remember?) Believe me, I have no inclination to do that. What I'd rather propose to you is to engage in an ongoing discussion about Christianity. I'd like to give you an opportunity to share with me all the reasons you have for not being a Christian, and I'd like you to give me the opportunity to share with you all the reasons why I am one.

Would you be willing to do this? I think, at the very least, it would be stimulating for both of us, and we'd get to know each other better. Having one's faith challenged — whatever faith one holds — is always a good thing. If it can't "stand the fire," a faith isn't worth holding — whether it is Christianity or atheism. So, in love, let's challenge one another. What do you say?

Sincerely yours, with hope,

Greg

14

PART I

QUESTIONS ABOUT GOD

CORRESPONDENCE 1

Why has Christianity done so much harm?

March 13, 1989

Dear Greg:

I received your letter yesterday and found it most thought-provoking.

Let me first say that I'm excited about your debate with the Islamic scholar and wish I could be there to see it. If it is possible, could you get me a tape of it? Let me know.

I find your idea of dialoguing about the subject of Christianity very interesting, and I'd be happy to do it. I've got enough time on my hands. I think you're giving me too much credit though, Greg. My belief (or lack of it) is not based too much on any positive position I hold, but rather, on a host of negative ones. I can find plenty wrong with most religious and political views, but I'm not at all firm on what I personally believe — at least not on religious matters. I really don't have a "faith" or "worldview" of any sort. I only know for sure what I *don't* believe. Also, unlike you, I'm not a trained philosopher, so if you write to me like you wrote in your dissertation, forget it! I won't be able to follow you. So you'll have to keep it simple.

As you know, I admire the education you've pursued, Greg, and I have often wondered how it is that you could continue to believe in this Christianity business in spite of the rather liberal institutions you've attended. It baffles me. I find the whole thing pretty implausible. But I've never been one to pass up an argument, so why start now?

You invited me to raise whatever objections come to mind, so I'll jump right in. Here's one I've wondered about a lot: how could an all-powerful and all-loving God allow the church to do so much harm to humanity for so long? Isn't this supposed to be His true church, His representation on earth? That's what I was taught in my Catholic days.

So I'm wondering, where was God when the Christians were slaughtering the Muslims and Jews — women and children included — during the "holy" crusades? Why did God allow "His people" to burn almost the entire population of Jewish "unbelievers" in Spain during the Spanish Inquisition? Why would an all-loving God allow the church to take part in something like the Holocaust (at best it looked in the other direction) — and do all these things "in His name"?

To my mind, this alone is quite enough to prove that the church does not possess any true philosophy. And it was this church, was it not, that decided which books were "divine" and should constitute the "Holy Bible." As far as I'm concerned, this is itself enough to reject the Bible as a joke.

Well, you wanted an objection: you've got one. I look forward to your response.

Give my love to Shelley and the kids.

Love always,

Dad

March 16, 1989

Dear Dad,

Thanks so much for your letter. About my debate, if I can get a tape for you, I certainly will. I know they have even videotaped these debates before (the man I'm debating has on file over 300 such videotapes!), but I don't know the plans of the Muslim association sponsoring this debate. I'll let you know.

I'm so happy you're willing and interested in having an ongoing discussion about Christianity. I can tell this is going to be engaging and stimulating for both of us. I know you are, as you said, much more sure about what you don't *believe than about what you* do *believe. That's fine. It's always easier to prove a false theory false than it is to prove a true one true, so it is reasonable to have more beliefs about what you think is false than about what you think is true. It's a sign of a healthy, critical mind.*

I would only ask that you try to keep an open mind as to the possibility of the truth of at least some of the central beliefs that Christianity has traditionally taught. My only claim — the one I want to attempt to defend — is that the foundational beliefs of Christianity are the most reasonable beliefs to base one's life on. The belief that there is a personal, loving God who is ultimately revealed in and through Jesus Christ, who has provided salvation by grace to the world through this man, and who has inspired the Bible as our means of learning of, and interacting with, Himself: these beliefs, I argue, are more substantiated, and far more fulfilling, than any other worldview one could hold. And my goal, quite frankly, is to convince you of the truth of these beliefs and bring you into a relationship with Christ. I know firsthand the fullness of life, the peace, and the joy that this relationship gives, and I want to share it with you. And, as you requested, I promise to keep my end of the discussion on a layperson's level.

Now the objection you raised in your last letter was a really good one. (I clearly am not, *as you humbly claim, giving you "too much credit.") My first and primary response is that I don't think God can be held responsible for what the Catholic Church — or any church, or any religion whatsoever — has done or shall do. From my perspective, the God whom the Bible talks about, and whom Jesus Christ incarnates, is a God of love, and this entails that He is a God of freedom, for you cannot have love without freedom. We were created with the ability to choose love, and thus with the potential to choose its opposite — evil.*

To assume that God is responsible for our evil — even the evil committed "in His name" — is, I suspect, to assume that humans are robots who simply act out a divine preplanned program. But if that were the case, we could never be loving beings. I want to argue that, ultimately, all evil in the world comes from free wills other than God. What God wills and does is always good. Whatever is not good has its origin from someone or something other than God.

The fact that it was the "Christian church" which chose to do the evils you write about, and to do them using God's name, in my mind only serves to show that all that goes under the name of "Christian" is not necessarily Christian. Christianity isn't a religion or an institution of any sort: it's a relationship. Within the religion of Christianity there are, and have always been, genuine Christians — people who have a saving and transforming relationship with Jesus Christ. And this fact accounts for the tremendous good Christianity has brought to the world (in spite of the evils). But the "religion" of Christianity, the "institution" of the church, is not itself Christian. Only people, not institutions, can be Christian.

Thus, I want to sharply distinguish between the Christianity I'm defending and the "Christian church": the two need not have anything more than a name in common. I wouldn't dream of trying to defend all that's been done under the label "Christianity." Like you, I am enraged by a great deal of it.

Well, thanks again for responding. I can't tell you how happy I am that we're openly dialoguing like this. Digest my response and give me your feedback. OK?

With love,

Greg

Why is the world so full of suffering?

March 23, 1989

Dear Greg:

Nice to hear from you so soon. I'm surprised you can keep up this fast a pace of letter-writing amidst your busy schedule. But I've got a good bit of time on my hands, so you set the pace. Like you, I'm enjoying the chance to air our thoughts.

Well, your distinction between the "Christian church" and "Christians" is interesting and novel, but frankly, I don't buy it. Isn't the church supposed to be God's delegated authority on earth, or is that simply a Catholic idea I picked up along the way? In any case, you would think that God would oversee at least *some* of its activities if it is to be His vehicle for saving the world.

But this is really just part of a bigger problem I have with the idea of an all-loving God. It's not just the evil in the church that's the problem, it's the evil in the whole world. If God created this world and cares about it, why is there so damn much suffering in it? In your letter your answer was that God can't be held responsible because He gave man the freedom to choose to do right or wrong. But, Greg, I don't feel that the question can be swept away so easily. When the freedom to decide to do harm results in pain and suffering to innocent people, God is simply not the "loving" God you make Him out to be!

I thought about this when I read about this lunatic down here in Florida who was released from jail after some seven or eight years for raping a teenage girl and then chopping off both her arms, leaving her for dead. It was his free choice to commit the crime, but what choice did the innocent girl have? It would appear that the "loving," protecting God forgot all about her! Why does God value the freedom of the criminal, but not the freedom of the victim?

Another situation along these lines is the drought in Africa causing millions of people to starve because of the lack of rain. There are no choices involved here. Nature just got fouled up in the water supply, so millions of people, all of them innocent, most of them children, die a horrible death. Where was the "loving and protecting" God during this, or did He just forget them? Or was God punishing them for some sins, or for being Muslim, like I've heard some bozo Christian evangelist say? That would be worse than a God who just forgets them!

The point is, this world doesn't look at all like the kind of world we'd have if there were an all-powerful, all-loving God behind it. And I don't see that your explanation of freedom improves the situation much.

Well, enough for now. Look forward to your letter.

Lots of love,

Dad

March 29, 1989

Dear Dad,

Well, Dad, I've got to admit that you are raising some extremely good points in your letters. You are raising the most difficult questions a theist can face. This is really good material.

Now, you're wondering how an all-loving God could allow a girl to get raped and mutilated by a sicko, and you don't buy the explanation that

22

God gave this sicko free will, for this explanation doesn't take into consideration the (violated) free will of the girl.

This is a very tough question, to the point where it's almost insensitive to even give an answer. And, indeed, under the emotional impact of this nightmare it would be perfectly understandable to be angry at God and everything else in the world. For those touched by this tragedy, rage is the only understandable immediate response. The Bible itself records the honest questions, and even angry prayers, of many "heroes of the faith" (e.g., Job, David, Jeremiah). God isn't threatened by our anger or doubts.

But when the dust eventually settles, there comes a time to begin to think through who is really responsible for this evil. And when we do this, my contention is that responsibility can't be attached to God.

It seems to me, Dad, that if God is going to give free wills to His creatures, He has to allow for the possibility of them misusing that freedom, even if this means hurting others. To be significantly free is to be morally responsible, and to be morally responsible means being morally responsible to each other. What is the freedom to love or not love unless it is freedom to enrich or harm another? God structured things this way because the alternative would be to have a race of robots who can't genuinely love — but that's hardly worth creating, is it?

So why doesn't God intervene every time someone is going to misuse his freedom and hurt another person? The answer, I believe, is found in the nature of freedom itself. A freedom which was prevented from being exercised whenever it was going to be misused simply wouldn't be freedom.

Look at it this way: if I give Denay five dollars, can I completely control the way she spends it? If I stepped in every time she was going to spend this money unwisely (according to my judgment), is it really her money at all? Did I really give her anything? If the only things she can buy with her money are things which I decide are worthwhile, is it really her money at all? Is it not rather still my money which I am indirectly spending through her?

So too, if God really gives us freedom, it must be, at least to a large extent, irrevocable. He must have, within limits, a "hands off" attitude toward it. God creates free people who can do as they please, not determined instruments who always end up doing what He pleases.

Well, I hope this sheds a little light on this sticky question. If I'm correct, the horrendous evil we see people inflicting on each other in this world is a necessary possibility if this is to be the kind of world where love is possible. Even God couldn't have it any other way. Let me know if, and how, you see it differently.

I look forward to your response.

As always, with all my love,

Greg

CORRESPONDENCE 3

Is the risk of freedom worth all the suffering?

April 8, 1989

Dear Greg:

I trust all is going well with you and the family. How is your Muslim debate shaping up? Sorry I was a bit slow in responding to your last letter, but it required a good bit of thought.

Your point about the relationship between freedom and responsibility may have something to it. It's most intriguing. But I have another nagging question. One has to question the wisdom of a Creator who would wager so much for freedom. Is it all worth it? To create a world in which mad men like Hitler or Stalin can use their freedom to take away the freedom — and the lives — of millions of others is, quite frankly, very poor management. If He values freedom so much, why the hell did God make it so tenuous that the will of one could destroy the freedom of millions?

Is the whole thing worth it? Freedom's nice, but I don't know if it's worth all the evil and pain we see in this world. I'm sure if we could ask that girl who was raped and mutilated, she'd say it *wasn't* worth it. If you could talk to the Jewish victims of Auschwitz, they'd say to hell with Hitler's precious free will. If you could talk to the Ethiopian mother of the kid dying as he tries to suck one more drop of milk from her dehydrated breast, I doubt she would say it was worth it.

Sorry to be such a tough nut, but it seems like a valid question.

Lots of love,

Dad

April 11, 1989

Dear Dad:

I appreciate the seriousness with which you're taking our correspondence. You're clearly putting a lot of thought into these letters, and I love it. Your question is certainly valid.

There are four points I'd like to discuss in response to your question. First, I would argue that the risk of freedom must be exactly proportional to its potential for good. If I have the freedom to love one person only, I have the freedom to hurt one person only. If I have the freedom to love them a little, I have the freedom to hurt them a little. If I can love them a great deal, I can hurt them a great deal. And so on.

The fact that we humans have such an incredible amount of potential for evil, then, is to my mind indicative of the fact that we also have an incredible amount of potential for good. Yes, there are Hitlers and Stalins in the world. But there are also the Ralph Walenbergs, the Mother Teresas, the Martin Luther King, Jrs. And I don't see how you could have the latter without at least risking the possibility of the former. If we have the potential to oppress or slay millions, it's because we also have the potential to liberate and love millions.

I can understand why you might see this as "bad management," and perhaps it would be if there were some other way of doing things. But I don't believe there is. In my view the proportionality between the possibilities of good and evil inherent in freedom is what's called a metaphysical truth. It's like the three sides of a triangle. If you have freedom, you have to have this risk.

So is it all worth it? This is my second point. Under the impact of nightmarish tragedy, it is certainly understandable that one might think not. But consider three things: first, in our own lives we all know that

26

love can hurt. In loving another person, in raising kids, in developing deep friendships, we often suffer a great deal. I know you've experienced your share of this in your own life. People reject us, they die, kids rebel, etc. And yet, we continue to love. We normally regard it as cowardly, as tragic, and as terribly unhealthy not to do so. If a person never loved, he'd never suffer. But then again, he'd never really live.

But isn't God in this same position, only on a cosmic scale? To refuse to create a world where love was possible because the risk was too great seems to be beneath God. Love is really the only reason worth creating! It's not freedom for the sake of freedom that God values — it's love. Freedom is simply the only possible means to this end.

This leads to my third point. From a Christian perspective, the risks involved in creation are not only, or even primarily, for human beings. God Himself risks a great deal in creating the world. The biblical perspective on God reveals a God who throughout history has suffered from the ill choices of human beings, and He suffers because He loves. In the Book of Hosea, God portrays Himself as one who is married to, and deeply in love with, a wife who will not be faithful. She harms herself, her husband, and her children by prostituting herself. So, with a great deal of pain, God continually attempts to call His people, His bride, back to a faithful relationship with Him.

In fact, so risky is the creation for God, according to Scripture, that it involved Him in becoming a human being and dying a hellish death on the cross. In spite of our rebellion against Him, God loved the world so much He was willing to go to this extent to have an eternal relationship with us. On the cross of Calvary, God took upon Himself all the sin of the world, and all the pain and punishment that that sin produces. He didn't have to. He did it out of love — because love is worth it. It's worth dying for, even in God's view.

And this leads to my fourth point. We need to ask the question of whether love is worth it from the broadest possible perspective. If this short life is all there is, if the suffering death of victims spelled the complete end of their existence, then perhaps we might legitimately argue that the risk is not worth it — at least not for the victims.

27

But if Christianity is true, this simply is not the case. Our earthly, temporal lives are but a brief prelude to a life that is going to go on forever. For a great many this life is indeed filled with nothing more than pain and suffering, but from an eternal perspective, this is only a small part of the whole story. Jesus died on the cross so humans could exist eternally in the peace and joy of God — heaven — and the promise of Scripture is that this state of being will be such that our present sufferings can't be compared to it (Rom. 8:18). In the light of Auschwitz, it must be incomprehensibly beautiful — which is exactly what Scripture says it is (1 Cor. 2:9).

If there is no heaven, Dad, then all the sufferings, tears, and cries of the dying children go unanswered. Life is finally tragic for all of us. All of our hopes, longings, strugglings, striving come to nothing, pure nothing! "Life's a bitch, then you die." But isn't there something in the depth of your heart which refuses to accept this as the whole truth? Isn't there something within you which resonates with the biblical proclamation that this story must have a happy ending?

I have a lot of reasons for believing in God, and a lot of reasons for believing that Christianity is true — things I hope to share with you some time in the future. But even apart from this, I simply refuse to accept that existence can be the senseless nightmare it appears to be, if in fact this short life is the only life there is.

I look forward to your reply.

I love you, Dad.

Greg

CORRESPONDENCE 4

Does God know the future?

April 17, 1989

Dear Greg:

It was good talking with you and Shelley the other day by phone. You sound pretty excited about your up-coming debate with the Muslim scholar. I am too. Be sure to let me know how it goes.

As I told you by phone, I really enjoyed your last letter. Your thoughts about heaven strike me as wishful thinking. Who said life "shouldn't" be as tragic as we find it? But your reflections on freedom, love, and responsibility are insightful. They raise a new question for me. Since God supposedly is all-knowing, why didn't He just look ahead and see who was and wasn't going to use freedom rightly, and then just create the good people? We'd still have freedom, but in a world without suffering. It strikes me as odd that God should have to take "risks" at all. Isn't He (in your view) in total control?

Chew on this and let me know what you think.

Love always,

Dad

April 29, 1989

Dear Dad:

Well, my debate with Dr. Badawi, the Muslim scholar, went very well. The auditorium was packed, especially with Muslims, and it was a real treat for me to share with them some of the reasons why I believe Jesus was God incarnate. The debate was really about the Trinity, but most of the time was spent talking about Jesus (since the two subjects are inseparable). As one might expect, all the Christians in the crowd I talked to thought my arguments were much more persuasive than his. But, I'm sure, the Muslims had the same feelings about Dr. Badawi. He was extremely sharp, but I feel good about my presentation and responses to him as well.

On to our debate now. Your question in your last letter about God's foreknowledge is a good one, but I think it's based on a misconception of what God's omniscience (His knowing everything) entails. In the Christian view God knows all of reality — everything there is to know. But to assume He knows ahead of time how every person is going to freely act assumes that each person's free activity is already there to know — even before he freely does it! But it's not. If we have been given freedom, we create the reality of our decisions by making them. And until we make them, they don't exist. Thus, in my view at least, there simply isn't anything to know until we make it there to know. So God can't foreknow the good or bad decisions of the people He creates until He creates these people and they, in turn, create their decisions.

Now I should tell you that this isn't the traditional Christian position. The traditional Christian understanding is that God does foreknow the free actions of everybody. But even here it is held that God foreknows them only because these people are, in fact, going to do them. God's knowledge is based on the people's (future) action, not vice versa. So it would be impossible for God to refrain from creating these people on the basis of their (yet future) action. Their future action wouldn't be there unless God did create them!

I personally think this last position is philosophically untenable. But both positions deny that God has a knowledge of the world which is independent of the actual world. Since God's knowledge is based on the created world, God isn't free to selectively create a perfect world on the basis of an imperfect world He supposedly knows about ahead of time.

My answer, I know, was a bit philosophical. And I promised you earlier to keep the discussion as much in "common language" as possible. But hey, your question was pretty philosophical — so what could I do?

Chew on that a while and let me know what you think.

With all my love,

Greg

CORRESPONDENCE 5

Why does God create earthquakes and famines?

May 11, 1989

Dear Greg:

I'm so glad to hear your debate with the Muslim went well. Please get me a tape of it if you can. A video would be even better. I'd love to see it.

Your last letter threw me for a loop. Not only did I have to read it several times to understand it, but what you're saying goes against a lot of what I was taught about God in my Catholic days. It seems like your view of God is much more "human" than what I've always thought God was supposed to be. I'm no authority on the Bible, but isn't God here seen as knowing the future? I admit your view sounds better than the standard one—I couldn't make sense of that at all!— but I wonder if your view is just your own creation.

In any case, you have explained adequately enough why God can't guarantee ahead of time that people won't misuse their free will. But there's another serious difficulty with your belief in an all-loving God which neither your view of freedom, nor God's knowledge, touches on. How do you get God off the hook for evils which don't arise from anyone's decision? Since God is the one who directly creates everything, why does He create famines, earthquakes, mud slides, AIDS, deformed babies, and the like? Surely no one's free will— except God's—can be blamed for these! If He's all-loving, one would think that He'd exercise a little more care with His creation.

Enough for now.

Lots of love,

Dad

May 29, 1989

Dear Dad:

Sorry I've been slow in responding to your last letter, but I've been really caught up in the "end of semester" madness here at Bethel. Let me first deal with the question of God's knowledge of the future, and then I'll try to address the issue of natural evil (evil in nature).

The view that God doesn't know future free actions is not just my own. A good many theologians hold to it. This view doesn't maintain that God doesn't know anything about the future. It only maintains that God doesn't eternally foreknow the free decisions people will make in the future. If there are aspects of the future which are already determined, either by present circumstances or by God's own will, these God would know for they are presently there to know. Future free acts, however, aren't. So the future isn't nearly as wide open to God as it is to us, but it is open to an extent. There are risks in creation, even for God.

Now as to whether or not this view is in the Bible: theologians, of course, disagree about this, but it is my conviction that this view is very biblical. I won't bore you with detail, but I find the God of Scripture to be interacting with people in a way that assumes that He faces the future with a certain degree of openness. The future is not an eternally settled matter. Thus, for example, God frequently asks questions of people in the Bible, and occasionally even changes His own mind in the light of new circumstances. (See Ex. 32:14; 1 Sam. 15:11; Jer. 18:7-10; 26:19.) This would, of course, be impossible if He had a fixed blueprint of all events ahead of time.

This open-ended view of God is, I suppose, more "human," but in my opinion it is so precisely because it's more biblical. The view of God as knowing and controlling the whole future from the beginning is in my estimation more the product of Aristotelian philosophy than it is the Bible.

On the issue of natural disasters, it is true that there is no human will which is directly at fault here. But does this mean that God is directly responsible for them? I want to argue that He's not. Consider three things, Dad.

First, I would argue that most of the pain and suffering in the world is the result of evil people, not nature, and that even the pain caused by most natural disasters could be minimized or eliminated if humans were what God created us to be. Take famines, for example. Do you think anyone would ever starve if everyone "loved his neighbor as himself"? I'm told by specialists in the field that there is more than enough food in the world to feed everyone. It's just that it's hoarded by a few who already have more than they need, at the expense of those who have less than they need. Americans, to be more specific, make up about 7 percent of the population of the earth, but we consume over half its resources! I'm told that the average first world person consumes as much over what they need as third world people consume under what they need.

Think how much "natural" evil could be prevented if there were no political wars (the Ethiopian tragedy clearly could!), if there were no arms race, if there were an equal distribution of the world's resources, if humans who had the means cared enough to invest in the safety and welfare of others? Even the floods in Bangladesh, I am told, are largely the indirect result of human apathy about our environment (e.g., screwing up the ozone layer) and about the welfare of the Bangladesh people (e.g., assisting them to build flood-proof housing).

So, Dad, I would argue that much of what appears to be a "natural" evil isn't always such. It arises from evil hearts.

Secondly, it may be that a good deal of what we call "evil" is simply due to the fact that anything which God could create would be limited in certain respects. The very fact that what God creates is less than Himself introduces limitations and imperfections into the picture. Any created thing must, for example, possess a limited set of characteristics which rules out the possibility of it possessing other characteristics incompatible with these. But this can lead to some unfortunate consequences. The rock which holds you up must also be hard enough for you to stub your toe on it. The air which you breathe must also be thin enough to allow you to fall through it when not supported by a hard surface. The water which quenches your thirst must also be dense enough so you can't breathe in it, and so on. The dependability of the world which makes it possible for rational, morally responsible creatures to live works against us in certain circumstances. Indeed, every positive feature of any created entity is a potentially negative feature in certain circumstances.

The limitations of reality, then, go hand in hand with the definiteness of reality. I don't really regard this as an inherent evil: it's just the way things have to be. I suspect that were it not for the fall of humanity we would be quite at peace with the limited, and sometimes unfortunate, nature of things.

But there yet remains at least some natural evil which doesn't seem due either to the limitations of the world or to the fact that people aren't as perfectly loving as they were created to be. Deformed babies, for example, aren't explained by either of these two explanations. How does a theist respond to these? This leads to my third consideration.

If the Bible is correct, Dad, human free wills aren't the only free wills which have been created. The universe is inhabited by innumerable spiritual free beings as well, beings which are not physical, at least not as we understand physics. I know this may seem like a ludicrous idea to you, Dad, but you should at least try to realize that this is a view which has been shared by almost every culture which has ever existed up to our own. Perhaps here our "enlightened" scientific mentality prevents us from understanding something other peoples have always understood.

The biblical term for these beings is "angels" or "demons" — but I don't want you to get the idea of winged, white harp players or red-horned pitchfork holders. There's nothing in the Bible about such silly notions.

They are also called "principalities" and "powers," which gives much more the impression of a "spiritual force" than an embodied entity.

In any case, the Christian understanding, based on Scripture, is that these entities are, like us, personal and free and, like us, some of them have used their freedom for evil. These evil spiritual forces — "demons" if you will — are now in a state of war against God and everything that is good, and the earth is (perhaps among other places as well) their battlefield. There is enough in Scripture to discern that these were beings whose potential for love was far above that of even human beings. But, correspondingly, their potential for evil was greater as well. Satan, as you may have heard, was once "Lucifer," the most beautiful of all God's creatures. I take that to mean he had the greatest capacity to love. Now, however, he is pure, undiluted evil. He is Hitler on a cosmic scale! And his power to influence, as well as that of other "demons," is vast (recall the love-responsibility correlation we talked about in our April 11 correspondence).

In the Christian view, then, the earth has been literally sieged by a power outside itself. There is a power of pure evil which now affects everything and everybody on the earth. The Creator is not the only influence any longer. This is why the earth can be so incredibly beautiful on the one hand, and so incredibly nightmarish on the other. We live, individually and collectively, amidst a contradiction of good and evil. The beauty of the world couldn't be here by indifferent chance, but the evil couldn't be here by good design. (That's what this "problem of evil" is all about.)

My claim, then, is that the earth is a battlefield. We are, like Normandy in World War II, caught in the crossfire of a cosmic battle. And on battlefields, as you know, all sorts of terrible things happen. In such a situation, everything becomes a potential weapon, and every person a potential victim. And thus the entire cosmos, the Bible says, is in a state of chaos (Rom. 8).

I would never for a moment pretend to understand exactly how these demonic forces screw around with nature — the Bible is completely silent on this score. But it is my deepest conviction that all evil which can't be *accounted for by appealing to the necessary limitations of the world or the evil wills of people is due to the will of such beings as these. In the end, we are all more or less casualties of war.*

Well, I suspect you may have found this last suggestion a bit hard to swallow. This certainly was my view of it at one time. I now accept it as true, however, because it is a biblical teaching, and I have a lot of reasons for thinking the Bible is true. It alone makes the existence of an all-loving, all-powerful God compatible with "natural evil." I have a lot of reasons for believing in this God as well. At some point I want to share these positive considerations with you as well as answer your questions.

I look forward to your feedback.

With hope,

Greg

CORRESPONDENCE 6

Why did God create Satan?

June 6, 1989

Dear Greg:

Wow! That last one was a doozy! As you suspected, I did find much of it pretty implausible. I can, I suppose, accept your stuff about the limitations of creation, but your devil business is far-fetched. Still, I admit, this world looks to me more like a "battle-field" than a work of art from the hand of an all-loving God. So if someone were going to believe in such a God, I think he'd have to believe in something like this "cosmic conflict" you talk about. But to me that is just one more indication that your view of God is all wrong.

In any event, I have some more questions about this if you haven't tired of me yet. First, I'm wondering how a graduate of Princeton and Yale like yourself can really believe in angels and demons and the like. The idea that there are invisible creatures who can do good or evil in the world frankly sounds like something out of a *Star Wars* or medieval superstition.

Another question I have is this: why would God create Satan in the first place? You'll probably say that it was Satan's free choice to be evil, but if he was created to be so wonderful, how could he make such a bad choice? Bad people make bad choices — that's what makes them bad. And good people make good choices — that's what makes them good. So if Satan was so good, how come he made such a bad choice and now, supposedly, does so much evil?

The same point applies to humans, now that I think about it. How come *all* of God's people who were originally created good are so bad? You tried to excuse God for natural disasters by

38

pointing out how unloving and uncaring humans are—and I agree—but now I'm wondering whether this excuse really works. After all, He created us, didn't He? He gave us our nature. So isn't He to blame after all?

One final thing comes to mind. I was taught in the Catholic Church that heaven is a permanent place. I mean, once you're in, you're in forever. But Satan was supposedly in heaven, wasn't he? Yet he fell. So do you think people may even choose evil once they get to heaven? And if not, why the hell didn't God just create us there in the first place and save everyone the pain of earthly life? I'm still wondering why God has to take risks, I guess.

It seems like every question just leads to ten more questions. Do you think we're getting anywhere, Greg? Not that I mind. My brain hasn't had to work like this for decades, and I enjoy it. But I wonder if you're going to tire of it. I'd certainly understand it if you did.

Lots of love,

Dad

June 18, 1989

Dear Dad:

Don't think for a minute that I'm tired of your questions. I am loving this! Even if I don't succeed in my undying effort to make a preacher out of you, I'll still regard our dialogue as having been more than worth whatever time and effort we put into it. But that's beside the point because I know that, sooner or later, you are going to believe. You'll see.

Well, on to your questions. First, I can understand how this "cosmic conflict" business could sound like Star Wars to you. It used to for me as well. Now, however, it makes a lot of sense. What, after all, is so implausible about the notion of "spiritual beings"? Why should the notion of a nonphysical, personal being be any more difficult than the notion of a physical, personal being? If beings with consciousness such as ourselves exist — a fact which is remarkable in and of itself — why rule out the possibility of other types of personal beings existing? I think what gives it the "feel" of being science fiction is all the stupid pictures of angels and demons we've seen. But what I'm talking about has nothing to do with these cartoons.

Look, isn't it the case that the more we know about the universe, the stranger it becomes? Quantum physics deals almost entirely with a realm of the universe — the sub-atomic realm — which is almost entirely invisible. Not only can't we see it, but we can't even conceptualize what a photon, neutron, quark, etc. might look like. We can only formulate their behavior with mathematical equations. In fact, most of reality we can't see! It always amazes me when I think that right now there are radio waves with voices and music going right through me. But you'd never know it unless you turned on a radio. So the notion that there could be beings which I can't see doesn't seem so outrageous to me.

Nor does it strike me as implausible that such beings could be good or evil. If the universe can be inhabited by moral beings of the physical type, why not beings of a nonphysical type?

Of course, I myself would never believe that such beings existed unless I had good reasons to do so. It is, I admit, a strange belief to hold in our modern culture. But I think I have good grounds for doing so. I have, I believe, really solid ground for believing that Jesus is the Son of God and that the Bible is God's Word. (We've got to get into these reasons at some point.) And so if these two sources of authority portray the world as being influenced by spiritual forces, my grounds for believing in these authorities also constitute grounds for believing in the existence of these spiritual forces.

Still, I owe it to you (and to me) to address the legitimate questions you raise about this belief even before we consider one's basis for believing the authorities which ground this belief. So here I go.

You have a whole series of very good questions which are closely related, so I'm going to try to answer them in one sweep. The central issue, I think, is how a good creation can choose evil. This lies behind your question about Satan's fall and about humans being so prone to sin. It also lies behind your question about heaven. In heaven, presumably, the inhabitants will be perfectly good and will, therefore, never fall. So why didn't God create us in this state to begin with?

The way I think about this matter is as follows. As I wrote in some earlier correspondence, love requires freedom. It must be chosen. And the greater the possibility of love, the greater the possibility of evil. I think we agree on this.

But I don't think this implies that love must forever *be a tenuous affair.* We tend to become the decisions we make. *The more we* choose something, *the more we* become that something. *We are all in the process of solidifying our identities by the decisions we make. With each decision we make, we pick up momentum in the direction of that decision.*

Just observing people can, I think, prove this point. I knew an old lady once who was the most ugly, bitter, mean-spirited person I'd ever met. As a young lady, however, I am told that she was beautiful, personable, and fun. But at the age of 19 her fiancé ran off with her sister three days before her wedding date. She was understandably humiliated and hurt. But what is most tragic is that she proceeded to choose to be hateful and unforgiving toward her sister and ex-fiancé the rest of her life. Though her sister was extremely sorry for what she had done and tried numerous times to make amends later on (over the course of 50 years!), this lady would never budge. And with each decision against love and forgiveness, she solidified herself in bitterness. Like all negative emotions which are entertained over a long period of time, her bitterness eventually colored her whole outlook on life. She became her hatred. She became her bitterness. The momentum of her decisions became irreversible. She no longer chose it; she couldn't now choose otherwise! All the good God originally intended her to be was consumed by the repeated course of hate she chose. What started as her decision eventually became her nature.

41

So it is, I believe, in every area of our lives. The more we choose something, the harder it is to choose otherwise, until we finally are solidified — eternalized — in our decision. The momentum of our character becomes unstoppable. We create our character with our decisions, and our character, in turn, exercises more and more influence on the decisions we make. It's in the nature of free, created beings, and I don't see how it could be otherwise. Life, I guess, is a lot like the proverbial snowball rolling down the hill.

What applies to evil also applies to love. There was a time when I had to choose to love Shelley, and there was a very good possibility that I would choose not to love her (and vice versa). It was, as it were, a "probation period" — call it "courting." But with each choice we made for love, the less choice for love we had to make. The less the possibility of not loving was present. And now, though my love for her is yet "freely chosen," it really is a part of my nature. And the snowball keeps on rolling.

Love must always start free — but its goal is to become unfree. *To be unable not to love is the highest form of freedom in love. (This is why God is perfectly free and yet, the Bible says, He "cannot sin." But being eternal, He never needed a "probation period" to get this way.)*

So as I see it, Dad, all the creatures which God creates to share love with must go through a "probation period" — a period in which they choose to love or not love. They could not just be created "in heaven." Once chosen, however, for whatever period of time is necessary (depending on their nature), they become solidified in their decision. This is what the Bible means by heaven and hell. It is the "eternalization" of one's character.

Lucifer, then, was the greatest of all creatures, not because of who he actually was, *but because of who he could* become. *His greatness lay in the magnificent potential for love which he had. But this also implied that he had an unthinkable potential for evil. And a decision started the difference. The difference between a Hitler and a Mother Teresa started somewhere with a small decision.*

This also was, in my view, the "goodness" of humanity as it was originally created. It's what the biblical account of Adam and Eve is all about. We had, and have, the potential to be beings of incredible love.

But that means we had, and have, the potential to be beings of incredible destruction. And we, to a large degree, make ourselves one or the other.

Let me close with this, Dad. The "snowball effect" which is true of individual lives is also true of societies and of humanity in general. What can be easily discerned with our eyes, and what the Bible clearly teaches, is that humanity is now a long way down the hill — in the wrong direction! You asked about how all of humanity could be so screwed up, and this is why. Evil tends to propagate evil, individually and societally. And this is part of what is meant in Christian theology by "original sin."

The message of Scripture, Dad, is that we are all, individually and collectively, too far down the road to now "make ourselves" what God intended us to be. We can't, on our own, make ourselves right with God, with each other, and even with ourselves! We need a new start, a new creation, a clean slate. And this, according to the Gospel, is what God has given us in Jesus Christ. He became a man, lived His life, and died on the cross to perfectly reconcile us with God and to give us a new life — God's life. And it's available to all who are willing to believe. The only way of becoming the being full of the life, joy, and peace which God created us to be — and the only way to be "eternalized" in this state — is by getting it as a gift. And this we get by entering into a relationship with Christ.

The reason why I could never grow tired of dialoguing with you about the faith, Dad, is that I want so much to see you enter into this relationship and to share in this new life.

I love you always,

Greg

Is your God all-powerful?

June 26, 1989

Dear Greg:

Well, I have to admit you have a knack for making the implausible sound halfway plausible. I'm clearly not catching you off guard with my questions. Not that I buy your "cosmic warfare" business, but I can at least see how a person could intelligently believe it. Your stuff about how we "solidify" ourselves with our decision seems to be true to life—a scary thought for a 70-year-old like myself—and it answers the question about how originally good people can go bad. I've often wondered about this when hearing of criminals who seemed to have it all going for them early in life. And then there are the "saints" who sometimes come out of horrendous backgrounds. It sort of makes sense now.

But every time I hear you go off on this free will business I'm nagged with this question: I always thought that Christians believed that God is all-powerful as well as all-loving. When Arlyle died, the priest attributed it to "the mysterious will of God." Mysterious indeed! It crushed me emotionally and left me with four motherless children to raise, and no means to do it! But aren't Christians always saying, in the face of tragedy, "God had a purpose"?

But you seem to be attributing all evil to the purpose of evil people and the devil. So where does God even fit in? If He fits in at all, you can't blame other people. And if you blame other people, He can't fit in. But then it seems like you have a God who has no control! What about all this "trusting God" stuff? If the world is worked out according to human free will (with some devilish willing thrown in), what good does it even do to believe

44

in God? You have a God who can't do anything about anything! What if He loses this "cosmic battle"?

So it seems to me as if the only God worth believing in is one in control. But a God who would be in control couldn't be all-loving, and so, again, wouldn't be worth believing in. It's kind of a Catch-22.

As always, I suspect you have an answer and look forward to hearing from you.

Love always,

Dad

July 5, 1989

Dear Dad:

I think I now know where my aptitude for theological thinking comes from — you! You really have an ability to see problems and get at the heart of crucial issues. You'd probably have to be a professor of theology like myself to appreciate just how rare that gift is!

Well, Dad, you asked me whether God was all-powerful, whether He was in control, and what good it is to believe in Him. Let me address these in order.

Is my God all-powerful? I want to answer yes and no. Let me explain myself. It is my view (which I believe to be biblical) that God is all-powerful in the sense that God originally possessed all power. Before Creation, God was the only being who existed, and thus had all the power there was. He could do anything, and nothing opposed Him.

But with the creation of free creatures, I maintain, God necessarily surrendered a degree of His power. Or perhaps it is better to say God delegated *some of His power. Our freedom is a little piece of "controlling power" lent us by God. In order to allow creatures to be free, then, God voluntarily gives us a portion of His power, and thereby surrenders His opportunity to "always get His way." I don't think it could be any other way, for freedom must entail that the free person can decide his own way — and it may not agree with God's way. It is utterly impossible for God to be always in control, and yet allow free beings to exercise some control. Thus, to the extent that God "lends" power away, He no longer utilizes it.*

However, what's important to realize, Dad, is that this "surrender" of control is completely a voluntary act of God. If there is a "limit" on God's power, it is only there by His decision, not some power outside of Himself. If God at some point can't do something (e.g., rid the world of a particular evil), it's only because He decided to create a world in which there would be times when He could do nothing. Only if some power outside God limited God could He properly be said not to be omnipotent (all-powerful). Thus, in my view, God is in essence all-powerful, though He now chooses not to be. And the reason is because He desires a creation which is capable of love, and thus must be free (have some "power" of its own).

Now, is God "in control"? Is there a divine purpose behind every event? My own view is again, yes and no. And I again need to explain myself.

Since it is God Himself who delegates how much power each creature has, God is, in this sense, "in control." He determines the parameters of our freedom within the flow of history which He directs, and in this sense God is always "in control." For this reason there is absolutely no chance that God could ever lose this "cosmic battle." As much power as Satan has, the ultimate purpose of God — to have a creation which shares love with Him — is never threatened.

However, God does not control each particular individual, for each person must be to some extent free. Hence, within the limits set by God, an individual may purpose to do things which are utterly at odds with God's ultimate purpose. Thus, when an individual inflicts pain on another individual, I do not think we can go looking for "the purpose of God" in the event. Of course, God allowed the event to occur because His ultimate purpose includes having free agents; and this freedom, as I argued in an earlier letter, must be irrevocable. But to "allow" something and to "purpose it" or "cause it" are two very different things.

I know Christians frequently speak about "the purpose of God" in the midst of a tragedy caused by someone else. There was a young girl this year at Bethel who was killed by a drunk driver, and a lot of students were wondering what purpose God had in "taking her home." But this I regard to simply be a piously confused way of thinking. The drunk driver alone is to blame for the girl's untimely death. The only purpose of God in the whole thing is His design to allow morally responsible people the right to decide whether to drink responsibly or irresponsibly.

So on to your final question. What good does it do to believe in God if He's not in total control of the world? A great deal could be said about this, Dad, but I'm running short on time. Perhaps we can pick it up again in a later correspondence. But to put it in a nutshell, it makes a world of difference!

First, the main business of this life, from a Christian perspective, is not this life at all, but the next. This physical life which is temporary is but a prelude and "probation period" for a life that will last forever. From this perspective (but only from this perspective), God's surrendering some power during this span of time to allow for a wonderful state of affairs that will never end in the next life makes sense. If this is not true, life is ultimately tragic and absurd.

In a similar vein, since God is yet in control of the cosmic scene, believing in God means having faith that all that God stands for — love, truth, justice, peace, etc. — will ultimately triumph. All of our basic moral convictions about how things should be will be answered. If this is not true, our moral aspirations are all ill-founded and result in futility. In this prelude period, evil may come to us from individuals that God does not control. But what God does control is the fact that this evil need not be the last word in our existence.

47

Another thing, Dad, is this: by believing in Christ as Savior, a person receives the fullness of life God always intended him to have, a fullness that no evil in the world can touch. The Apostle Paul tells us that "nothing can separate us from the love of Christ" (Rom. 8:35). Death itself does not touch it. Christ allows for freedom in the physical, public sector; but in the heart that allows Him to be such, He is total Lord!

Finally, while God has given humanity and other spiritual beings a great deal of freedom, He has not come close to surrendering all control to them. He is, even in this present, prelude period, still the most powerful being, even if He does not, by His own decision, exercise all power. God still exercises the dominating influence in this world, and He only knows what this world would be like without His constant, holy influence.

I hope this adequately addresses your questions. I really congratulate you on your theological astuteness. Please keep it up!

Your loving son, with hope,

Greg

CORRESPONDENCE 8

Why believe in God in the first place?

August 4, 1989

Dear Greg:

Sorry it's taken a while to get back to you, but I've been pretty tied up as head of the Kingswood Manor Home Owner's Association. Plus, your last letter was pretty dense (you're getting philosophical on me!) and it took quite a bit of work to digest it. All your "yes and no" answers . . . you talk like a damned theologian!

Here's the deal, Greg. You have really good answers to all my questions, and I admit that you've to some extent cleared away some of my obstacles to believing in the Christian God, but it's starting to feel sort of like a game to me. You have all these excuses to get God off the hook, and they're pretty impressive excuses; but it seems to me that the burden of proof is on anyone who claims to believe in an all-loving God to show that such a God exists. If you have to do all these theological gymnastics to preserve your faith, maybe it's because your faith is wrong! If God exists, why isn't He more obvious? I could invent a thousand reasons why we can't ever see the man on the moon, but sooner or later a person should suspect that maybe it's because there isn't a man there!

So I can see how all your material is convincing to a person who already believes in the Almighty, but I'm not quite in that position. I've always been inclined to believe that there must be some sort of "higher power" behind everything, but I don't see any evidence that it's a personal being who is all-powerful (in any sense) or gives a rip about humanity. In fact, I don't see how we can claim to know anything about it at all. Maybe we should have dealt with this first, but I told you before I don't have any set positive system of beliefs. I just raise the questions as they come to me.

So there you have it. Look forward to your response. |

Lots of love,

Dad

August 21, 1989

Dear Dad:

Well, the girls have apparently inherited a fair share of "Boyd stamina." I took them with me to several races the last few weeks, and they did great! Denay twice won the "12 and under" half-mile race, and Alisha came in third in both. It gives them a charge to beat boys, especially ones that are older than they are. Even Nathan got in on the act, though I don't think he had a clue as to what the whole thing was about. He just pretended to be "Superboy" and flew around the course with both his arms straight out in front of him. It's at times like these that I really wish you were up here. I think you'd really get a kick out of it.

Well, it sounds like we're getting down to the nuts and bolts of our theological discussion. Why believe in God in the first place? I have a lot of reasons, Dad. Some of these come from the head, while others come from the heart. Some involve very sophisticated philosophical reasoning, while others come "straight from the gut." But I think I can sum them all up in one straightforward argument. I call this "the anthropological argument" because it tries to demonstrate the existence of a personal God from the personal nature of human beings. I'll share with you the essence of this argument, and I'll try to keep it as non-technical as possible.

My basic line of reasoning is this: we human beings are personal beings. This means, I believe, that we are constituted by a mind which is self-aware and is rational, a heart which is free and can love and which is, therefore, morally responsible, and a soul (or call it what you will) which longs for meaning and significance. Consciousness, rationality, love, morality, and meaning: these, I maintain, constitute the essence of what it is to be a person in the full sense of the term.

Now the dilemma we face is this: either we exist in an environment (viz. the cosmos) which is compatible with these attributes, or we do not. Either our environment is congruous with these attributes — it renders them intelligible and answers them — or it does not. To illustrate, we hunger, and behold, there is food. We thirst, and behold, there is water. We have sex drives, and behold, there is sex. Our environment, then, is congruous with our natural hunger, thirst, and sex drive. And given the kind of world we live in, we can understand why we hunger, thirst, and have sex drives. Our cosmic environment "answers" our natural drives and thereby makes sense of them. Are you following me?

Well, the question is, does our cosmic environment answer to the basic features of our personhood outlined above? My contention is that unless our environment is ultimately itself personal, unless the ultimate context in which we live is self-aware, rational, loving, moral, and purposeful, then our cosmic environment does not at all answer to our personhood. In other words, unless there is a personal God who is the ultimate reality within which we exist, then we humans can only be viewed as absurd, tortured, freaks of nature; for everything that is essential to us is utterly out of place in this universe. This, on the one hand, renders human nature completely unexplainable. How could brute nature itself evolve something so out of sync with itself? And, on the other hand, it means that human existence, if we face up to our real situation, is extremely painful. We are the product of a cruel, sick, cosmic joke.

So, for example, we humans instinctively assume that reality should be rational, and that reasoning gets us closer to truth (and science seems to say that this assumption is valid), but in the end nature is irrational. There is no overarching mind to it.

51

We humans instinctively assume that love is a reality, that it is the only ideal worth living for and dying for. But nature seems to be an indifferent, loveless, brute process of colliding chemicals — and so our ideals are reduced to reacting hormones.

We humans instinctively assume that our moral convictions are true to reality, do we not? There are, of course, people who say that moral convictions are "just a matter of taste," but cut them off at an intersection and their convictions change. You did a gross injustice!

And we humans instinctively hunger for meaning and purpose. You can see it all around in the way people behave. We strive to infuse our lives with some sort of significance, some sort of meaning. But if our cosmos is ultimately indifferent and purposeless, all we are, all we do, all we believe in, all we strive for is "dust in the wind." After we exist, it matters not whether anyone has ever, or ever will again, exist. Everything is ultimately meaningless.

So, unless the ultimate source of all existence is at least as personal as we are, Dad, my contention is that who we are is both unexplainable and extremely hard to swallow.

Perhaps I have condensed this argument too much, but I don't want to be guilty of overkill here. So why don't you let me know what you think of my thoughts here, and maybe your questions will flush out the nuances of my argument.

Take care, Dad. I love you,

Greg

CORRESPONDENCE 9

Couldn't it all be by chance?

September 15, 1989

Dear Greg:

It was good to talk to you the other day. Again, I'm happy to hear that the kids are enjoying these sporting events. I would like so much to be a part of that. If I were a good bit wealthier than I am, it wouldn't be a problem. But such is life.

Now, about your "Anthropological Argument." Greg, I may be misunderstanding you, but I simply don't see your point too well. It almost sounds like you're saying that there must be a God or life is a bitch. But hey, life *is* a bitch! So while I can agree that there's a part of us which would like to have a loving "Father in heaven" — it's a comforting thought I suppose — I don't see that this is more than wishful thinking.

You then say that humans aren't explainable unless there's a personal being who created us, but couldn't we just have come about by accident? Isn't that what the biologists tell us? Doesn't evolutionary theory say that our minds and morality are just part of our survival drive? I'm not even sure what I think about the theory itself, but it's an alternative explanation.

But again, I'm not denying some kind of force greater than ourselves lying behind the universe. I've always thought there is too much design in the cosmos to be all by accident. This world doesn't seem to be the kind of thing that could just pop into existence. But I just don't see how you can be sure that humans are as significant to this force as the Bible makes them out to be. Maybe we're just sort of a by-product to the whole show. The universe, after all, is a very big place! Our earth is less than a grain of sand on the cosmic beach. So much for my poetry!

53

Keep up the running and the writing. I find your letters to be most thought-provoking. I read them a number of times before I write my own.

Lots of love,

Dad

September 25, 1989

Dear Dad:

OK, you believe there is some kind of "force" which must be the cause of things. I'm just trying to inquire into what this "force" must be like. Now since an effect can't be greater than its cause, doesn't the fact that humans (the effect) are personal mean that the cause (the force) must also be personal?

The theory of evolution, if it is true, can only give us a biological guess as to how humans came about. But the more fundamental question is how evolution produces the kind of results it does in the first place. What must the ultimate "force" of the universe be like for evolution to have the kind of characteristics it has? I'm asking something about the process itself. This is a metaphysical question (meta = above). Science can't address it.

Now my argument, in a nutshell, is that the process itself can't be pure chance. Look, the only way we can understand why our minds can understand physical reality in the first place is by believing that the physical universe is "mind-like." Our thinking about reality presupposes that there is a correspondence between our mind and reality. Science operates with this assumption. This is what Einstein called "the incomprehensible comprehensibility" of the universe. How is it, for example, that his theory of relativity, worked out strictly with mathe-

54

matical formulas, "fits" reality? The success of his theory — which has since been demonstrated empirically (by experiments) — means that physical reality has the kind of mathematical structure Einstein worked out. Einstein didn't impose his theory on reality: he discovered it. The world was "mind-like" before a mind like Einstein's ever came along to see it.

But chance, Dad, simply can't produce mathematical formulas. And chance can't produce organisms like our minds that can know and work out mathematical formulas. Look at it this way: if our minds are simply "chemicals in motion," then any truth we think we may discover amounts to nothing more than a brute chemical reaction, and thus can have no more truth than, say, a burp. Chemical reactions are all equal on this score, regardless of how complex they are. So Einstein was just giving a complex burp with all of his theorizing.

But why then does his theory work? The success of his formula, and of all science, confirms our instinctive assumptions about the mind: our mind is more than a network of chemical reactions. It can rationally comprehend physical aspects of the world because the world is rational. And since you can't have rationality without a rational mind — you can't have it by sheer chance — there must be a rational mind behind the physical world. Your "force" must be rational.

I'd say the exact same thing about morality. If morality is simply the result of chance, what a certain species of primates needed to help them survive, then our moral claims have no objective reference point. They don't say anything about the way things are, only about the way we (by accident of evolution) feel.

But when you say that Hitler was "wrong" for slaughtering 6 million Jews, or when you say that that lunatic guy you wrote me about was "wrong" for mutilating that girl, you mean more than just "you don't like how it feels." Don't you assume that these deeds contradict the way things ought to be? Aren't you making a claim not about the way you are, but about the way the universe is? Aren't you assuming there is a moral law in the universe, in the very structure of things, which these idiots have violated?

What is very important to see, however, is that chance, sheer chemical reactions, can be no more moral than they can be rational. And since the effect cannot be greater than the cause, the "force" which lies behind the cosmos must not only be rational: it must be moral.

And now the "it" is starting to look a whole lot like a person.

The same thing can, I believe, be said of our self-awareness. We are self-aware, conscious, and this is why we are free. But can chance chemical reactions, however complex they may be, ever be free? So with love. So with meaning.

What I was saying about how unbearable it is to be a person in an environment which is fundamentally impersonal was not meant to argue for the existence of God on the basis of wishful thinking. It was rather meant to argue that it is incongruous with everything else we know about the world to suppose that nature could produce creatures which have longings which nature doesn't itself fulfill. This would be to assume, once again, that the effect outruns the cause, and in a disastrous fashion. If the ultimate canvas against which the cosmos is painted is not personal like we are, then we are very much like fish out of water. We desperately cry out for water, but there never was such a thing as water! But how could such a state of affairs ever come about? Where did our longing for something that never existed, and that never could exist, come from?

My point, then, is that the characteristics of personhood, and the longings which arise from personhood, require that the ultimate cause and context of personhood is personal. This, at least, is the only rational assumption to make about "the force."

Let me say one final word, Dad, about why I believe in God. I really do feel that this argument (and many others like it) is valid. In a sense, I feel like it is simply consistently drawing out the implications of what all of us believe about ourselves and the world anyway. But my belief in God isn't a mere theory which I happen to hold to be true. It is a relationship.

When I came to believe in God, and came to trust in the sacrifice of Jesus Christ as the only way I could be made right with this "moral force" I must someday answer to, I discovered by experience that the longings of personhood do have "an answer." I was a dried-up fish that discovered there actually was water! And what wonderful, refreshing, and fulfilling water it was! All that the heart longs for is not only given an explanation by a faith in God: they are given their fulfillment. *My hope, Dad, is that someday you will not only agree with my theory, but share in this relationship.*

I very much look forward to your response.

Your loving son,

Greg

Why didn't God spare your mother?

October 18, 1989

Dear Greg:

Well, I've got to hand it to you, that's a pretty persuasive argument you've got there. I've never heard anything like that before. Is it your creation? The whole notion that our personal characteristics had to come from somewhere and are rooted in something makes sense to me. I found your stuff about morality and reason particularly convincing.

So, my "force" has personal characteristics. But I'm not sure how far that's gotten us, Greg because I don't see what difference it makes what characteristics God has: He still doesn't seem very interested in us! And what good does believing in a God with person-like characteristics do if He's not personally interested in you or me? I don't mean to beat a dead horse, but if He was as personally interested in us humans the way you born-again types say He is, I simply don't see how He could let us go down the course we've gone down for so long.

Just think about it, Greg: do you know how easy it would have been for God to simply snuff out Hitler and save the lives of all those Jewish children? Why not just abort the bastard before he's born? Or give him a fatal disease when he's a kid. Hell, it happens all the time. Why not to him?

And here's another aspect of religion I've never understood: prayer. If God is personally interested in us, as you say, we presumably can talk to Him. But does He listen? I don't think so. Think how many millions of Jewish parents banged God's ear off during the Holocaust? All they got was silence. Where was His personal concern then? The Bible has it that He saved them from the Egyptians by parting the Red Sea. But this time He seems to have been preoccupied with other more pressing issues.

So if God is personally interested in us, why is prayer so totally unsuccessful? I fail to recall any time in my life where the prayers of anyone were really answered. Tony used to always say that Leona and Grandma Raz were "powerful pray-ers." I always wondered what made them "powerful," because their prayers seemed pretty powerless to me. Leona lumped her prayers into novenas and prayed until her knees gave out. And I always felt her success in getting God's attention and getting her prayers answered were just about the same as the odds of chance.

When Arlyle was dying, we all prayed till we were blue in the face. Even you kids prayed. Maybe God doesn't listen to the prayers of sinful adults, but He should have at least heard the cries of you kids! Instead, you kids were left motherless and that set in motion a rather unfortunate history you yourself know only too well. If God had been personally concerned about us, Greg, He'd have spared your mother and spared all of us a tremendous amount of pain.

You can try to explain this, I suppose, with your cosmic warfare theory, but it seems easier to simply conclude that He doesn't give a damn. Whatever His personal agenda is in the universe, I don't see that it has a whole lot to do with our little earth.

There you have it, straight from the gut.

All my love,

Dad

November 23, 1989

Dear Dad:

I really appreciate the honesty of your last letter. It clearly was, as you said, a letter "straight from the gut." I think it deserves a response of the same caliber.

I think it's important to arrive at as much understanding of God and our world as we can, but there comes a time when the understanding either comes to an end or is incapable of addressing the depth of the issues we struggle with. A husband and father who lost his wife and mother of his children during the bombing of (say) Dresden may have an intellectual answer as to why the bombs were dropped, but this doesn't assuage his rage over the fact that it was his wife, and mother of his children, who was killed. I think, Dad, that you are in just this situation.

So what can I say? I can only speak "from the gut." I too have often asked God why my mom died. And I too have never received an answer. And I too have raged. God's not offended by this. It's just honesty, and God loves honesty.

Like every kid, I grew up with a need to feel unconditional love and acceptance from a mom, but this I never felt. As you know, sometimes we kids got the opposite message from our stepmother.[1] I always knew you loved me — and I remember always feeling "safe" when you came home — but your job took you away from the home most of the time. So, looking back on it, I can see that I grew up with an acute sense of abandonment. The full force of the pain of this didn't even hit me until I was an adult. Kids block out what they cannot bear.

But around the age of 20, after being a Christian for about three years, I received something that was far more important than an answer to my question "why": I received healing (and I'm still receiving it). Many memories from my childhood began coming back to me — usually in times of prayer — and they were sometimes extremely painful. I was, I guess, now healthy enough to deal with them. But in the face of these the Lord brought love and healing.

60

In the face of many of the things I interpreted as a kid as being a negative commentary on my self-worth (e.g., some of my stepmother's aberrant forms of punishment), the Lord showed me that I am lovable and infinitely precious in His eyes. And He caused me to experience this. In the face of the abandonment I experienced, the Lord said to me, "I will never leave you or forsake you" (Heb. 13:5). And in the face of my need for the unconditionally loving mother I never had, the Lord said, "I want to be that mother to you." And "He" is! Christ isn't our adversary in times of suffering: He's our cure.

Christ became that for me. My soul was, and is, filled with the unconditional love of Jesus. And unconditional love is the only life source for the soul and the only medicine for its wounds. An intellectual answer could never do that. My question still remains, but Christ has won my trust in Him by showing me His beauty—the beauty of a love, a grace, a tenderness, a gentle strength which no mere human being could ever match. He won my love and trust through the healing compassion of His eyes and the warm understanding of His embrace. He provided an understanding in the heart which the mind could never grasp. (That's why the Bible says that God gives believers a "peace that passes all understanding.")

What I also experienced, Dad, and what is shown throughout the New Testament, is that Jesus suffers with us in our suffering. That's how He heals us of our suffering. One of His names in the New Testament is "Immanuel," which means "God is with us." However low we sink, God is with us. He's there at the bottom waiting for us! He isn't off on some distant planet, indifferent to our plight. He's in the midst of all we go through.

You may remember that my first year in college I went through a long period of acute doubt over the truth of Christianity. This problem we've been discussing—the problem of evil—was at the heart of it. I was torn between two opposing convictions. The world, with all of its beauty, design, intricacy, and personal characteristics, demands that there must be a God. But, I thought at the time, the suffering of the world says that there can't be a God. It all came to a head for me one cold February night as I was walking back from an astronomy class at the University of Minnesota. Thinking of the grandeur of the stars we had just been looking at, I was saying to myself "there must be a God." But thinking of the nightmarish suffering of Auschwitz, I was saying to myself "there can't be a God." The two thoughts were battling with each other at hyperspeed. I was tormented.

Finally, just as I approached my car, I looked up to the sky and cried out with a loud, angry voice — "the only God I can believe in is one who knows firsthand what it's like to be a Jewish child buried alive, and knows what it's like to be a Jewish mother watching her child be buried!" And just then it occurred to me (or was it revealed?): that is exactly the kind of God Christianity proclaims. There is no other belief which does this. Only the Gospel dares to proclaim that God enters smack-dab into the middle of the hell we create. Only the Gospel dares to proclaim that God was born a baby in a bloody, crap-filled stable, that He lived a life befriending the prostitutes and lepers no one else would befriend, and that He suffered, firsthand, the hellish depth of all that is nightmarish in human existence. Only the Gospel portrait of God makes sense of the contradictory fact that the world is at once so beautiful and so ugly.

I guess what I'm saying, Dad, is this. I don't know exactly why God didn't answer our prayers for Arlyle. I know that if it wasn't for human sin, and if we weren't involved in this spiritual war, this painful situation never would have arisen. But more important than this explanation is this understanding: God was suffering with you, and me, and Arlyle, throughout the whole affair. He cries too. And through His participation in our pain, He wants to redeem it. He wants to bring about whatever healing is possible to you, and to me, and to all involved. His healing strength is in His vulnerability to pain. He's begun to bring about this healing in my life. He can do it in yours as well.

If you could just get a picture of the beauty of Christ in your mind, Dad, He'd win your love in a way reasons could never do.

Again, thanks for your honesty.

With love and hope,

Greg

---

[1]My father and stepmother were divorced in 1970. Jeanne Boyd is my second stepmother.

CORRESPONDENCE 11

Why would an all-powerful God need prayer?

December 15, 1989

Dear Greg:

I trust you all are getting into the holiday spirit. With three kids in the house, it's hard not to. I recall those Christmas mornings when you guys were all young. Those are some very fond memories. There's nothing quite like it. You don't know how much I wish I could be up there with you guys during this time of year. "I'm dreaming of a white Christmas" — down here in 80 degree Florida! Tell the little ones their presents are on the way.

Well, Greg, to be frank, I don't know what to do with your last letter. I too appreciate your "gut" honesty. I confess that I am touched by what your faith has done for you. And your view of God is moving (especially around this time of year). I'm wondering why, if your view is the Christian view, have I never heard it before? I think that when most people think of God, they think of this rather nasty, strong, old, bearded fellow above the clouds. You give quite a different scenario. But how does your view fit with the story of God destroying all of Sodom and Gomorrah, His killing off the Canaanites, and His sending the Flood over the whole earth? In the light of these tales, the nasty view of God seems more accurate.

In any case, I like your view, Greg. But I simply can't share your faith in it. I just have too many questions. Not to get too "academic" again, but if you'd like, I'd like to kick around the issue of prayer some more.

As I said before, I don't see that prayer ever works. Not only this, but I don't see how prayer ever *could* work. If God is all-good and all-powerful, and concerned about us, doesn't He already want the best for us? And so wouldn't He already be doing as much as He can ever do for us? So what are you asking for in prayer? For Him to care more? He supposedly already cares as much as He could. Are you asking Him to do more? He's supposedly already doing everything He can. Are you informing Him of some problem so He'll do something about it? He supposedly already knows everything. So you can't inform Him about anything, you can't coax Him to do anything, and you can't empower Him to do anything. So what the hell are you doing when you pray! The whole thing seems like a total waste of time to me.

I look forward to hearing from you. Have a wonderful Christmas. Give my love to Shelley and the kids.

Love always,

Dad

December 28, 1989

Dear Dad:

Thanks for your letter. Hope you and Jeanne had a nice Christmas. Ours was a lot of fun — and stress! With all the different relatives up here, the kids actually had four Christmas celebrations, all with a new set of presents, and all in one day! But you're right in your last letter: kids make Christmas magic, and it's all worth the work (and money).

Now on to your question about prayer. The main purpose of talking to God (that's all prayer really is) has little to do with asking for things, Dad. It's to build a faith-filled, loving relationship with our Creator and Redeemer. What kind of relationship would I have with Shelley if the only time we ever talked was to make requests of each other? Not much of one, I suspect. And so it is with God. The main function of prayer is simply to be with Someone you love: to talk, to listen, or to simply "commune" with your Creator.

A lot of the time when I pray I simply get a picture of Jesus in my mind and let Him say to me what He wants to say to me, things I need to hear. I let Him remind me of my worth and lovability in His eyes because of what He's done for me on Calvary. I let Him give me an experience of His love, and therefore of my worth. I let Him begin to revamp some of the negative tapes I got in my mind in the course of growing up. I let Him heal my memories. That is how all the growth in the Christian life takes place — from healing on the inside, from resting in God's love.

Asking for things — what's called "petitionary prayer" — is simply one minor aspect of this total relationship. It's not that God needs our petitions to be informed or empowered to do anything. You're right: He's already as good, as concerned, as informed, and as powerful as He can be. But because a loving relationship with Him is His highest agenda for us, He constructs the order of things such that a loving relationship with Him will be facilitated. And thus He ordains that some things will only be done through prayer.

It might help to look at it this way. Because God has love as His highest agenda, He gives us some "say-so" in the universe. We must have this if we are to be self-determining persons, and He must have self-determining persons in His creation if He wants love to be the creation's goal. We've already talked about this. So we humans have a good deal of power to determine the outcome of things, to have some "say-so" in our little corner of the universe.

Petitionary prayer is simply the spiritual aspect of the "power to influence" that God gives us. In the same way that God ordains that He will not do everything He'd like to do on a physical level — in order to give us freedom — so too He ordains things so that He will not always do what He'd like to do on a spiritual level. And He gives us this spiritual "say-so" for the same reason He gives us "say-so" on a physical level: to facilitate our freedom, our personhood, and thus a real, loving relationship with Him.

A genuine relationship, I believe, can only occur where there is personal interaction between two persons, where there is "give and take" between both parties. In other words, any genuine relationship requires that both parties are to some extent empowered over and against the other. This is as true in our relationship with God as it is in our relationships with other people. God doesn't want to be the only one calling the shots. Monopoly by one person — even if that "person" is God — always squashes the personhood of others. So God ordains things so that we are to some degree empowered in our relationship with Him. He ordains things so that we can actually influence the Creator, not because He needs us, but because He wants us. And petitionary prayer, in my view, is the principle means of this human-to-divine influence.

I think this addresses your question concerning how prayer could work. But, in honesty, it doesn't address the objection you raised that prayer does not in fact work. Let me say just a few things about that.

First, Dad, given the complexity of reality, I think it would be virtually impossible to "test" the effectiveness of prayer. I know of several published experiments done in hospitals to "test" the effectiveness of prayer (concluding that there is a positive correlation between prayer and healing), and while I find these tests intriguing, I doubt anyone who didn't already believe in prayer would find them very convincing. There are simply too many variables. There is no answered prayer that can't be chalked up to coincidence, and no unanswered prayer that can't be explained away.

But maybe this is as it should be. If petitionary prayer could be conclusively "verified," it would turn God into a sort of cosmic vending machine. Make your requests, pull the lever, and abracadabra, you have your wish granted. But this defeats the whole purpose of prayer which is to facilitate a faith-filled relationship with the Creator. So it takes faith to pray, and faith to see the answer to prayer.

Secondly, I'd again reiterate that, far more important than knowing the mechanics of unanswered prayer is knowing that God's on your side even when the prayer is unanswered. Perhaps we can think of it this way. Let's say there was a little house inhabited by American allies on Normandy beach when D-day broke out. In fact, let's suppose that the family in this unfortunate beach cottage consisted of the son, daughter-in-law, and grandchildren of the head captain of the invading American fleet. There they were, caught in the crossfire of this terrible battle. Let's say they had a radio line with this captain and could radio their requests to him during the battle. They told him they were being hit both with enemy fire and with American fire. They told him they were wounded and needed supplies, hungry and needed food, etc.

Now the captain cares a great deal about his son and his family and would like to answer every one of their requests. But, at the same time, there is a larger battle to fight, thousands of other lives to consider, and the outcome of this important battle which must be of preeminent importance. So sometimes this captain can meet his son's requests. But other times, given the strategic warfare of the enemy, he cannot. And perhaps sometimes their requests are not even to their own advantage given the course the battle is taking.

But the unfortunate family in the beach cottage doesn't have this broader perspective. They only know that the captain is on their side, that their requests are heard and are taken into account, and that sometimes their requests are granted and sometimes not. But they, lacking his stategic perspective, have no idea why this is the case. They don't have a purview of the whole battle. Their perspective is limited to the tiny windows in their cottage.

This is, I think, analogous to our relationship with God in our present fallen condition. There are undoubtedly billions of variables that go into God's moment by moment interaction with the world. There is His overall plan for humankind and for the cosmos. There is the necessary degree of freedom of each individual, human and angelic, with which to contend. There is His plan for each individual. There is the sheer number of opposing forces and allied forces available to consider. There is the strategy of the battle with which He is involved. There is the degree to which He has ordained our prayer to have consequences in the world to consider. And so on. And we know less than nothing about any of this! Our perspective is extremely myopic. We know infinitely less about the cosmic warfare we are involved in than that family in the cottage knew about the battle they were caught in.

In truth, we only can know this one thing: our Captain is in love with us, He wants the best for us, He's on our side, He hears and is influenced by our petitions, and when it is possible to promote the good and avoid pain, He does it. But in warfare this is simply not always possible — even for God — so long as He sticks to His highest agenda which is love and therefore freedom.

So why didn't God spare Mom? Honestly, Dad, over and above the general observation that this world is incredibly screwed up because of this cosmic warfare, I haven't got a clue. I'll find out someday. "We now see through a very dark glass," the Bible says. But, I believe, we can see enough to know that our requests are taken into account and to continue believing in the goodness and wisdom of the Captain we're talking to. And this, I think, is far more important, far more healing, than knowing the exact mechanics of why we, and Mom, had to suffer.

I hope this speaks to the issue you've raised. I'd encourage you, Dad, to begin talking to God, even if it's to express anger and disappointment with Him. The Bible is full of prayers like that. God isn't offended by them. If He were, they would not have found their way into His inspired Word! This kind of complaining, angry prayer can be healing in your life. Since you believe that God is personal, you must believe that He at least hears what you're saying. And to communicate at all — anything! — is the beginning of a relationship with Him.

Hope to hear from you soon.

With love and hope,

Greg

CORRESPONDENCE 12

Why would God care about us little humans?

January 14, 1990

Dear Greg:

It was good to talk to you last week on the phone. Thanks again for the touching card and flowers to Jeanne and myself. Hope Alisha is over her flu bug and that the rest of you are surviving your ungodly January weather up there. When are you guys going to finally wise up and move somewhere where you don't have to wear seventeen layers of clothes half the year?

Well, as I told you over the phone, your stuff on prayer made some sense to me. But like I said, I would think it would help whatever purpose the Almighty has for prayer if He'd at least occasionally show us that He hears us at all, that prayer has some positive effect on things. I can appreciate His not wanting to be a "cosmic vending machine," but I think He's erring in the opposite direction! Tell Him my gripe next time you talk to Him.

In any event, I have trouble with the whole idea of talking to God so long as I am nagged with the idea that we aren't central, or even important, to anything He's doing. I grant that the almighty force behind the creation has personal characteristics, but I'm still not convinced that this has any bearing on us. His "agenda," as you say, seems to be with something else in the universe. It seems to me that we are an accidental feature to the whole thing.

You talk a lot about God suffering for us. But why would God suffer the way you say He does for creatures as insignificant as us? I could see how people believed this back in the Middle Ages when they thought the earth was the center of everything. But we now know that the earth is this little insignificant planet, in a relatively small solar system, in a relatively small galaxy, which is located nowhere in particular in an incomprehensibly large universe. So what's the big deal about us? Why couldn't it be that He has a purpose for the universe, but we are simply not part of it? Is there anything to suggest that we are that important, or important at all?

I've got a few more questions on my mind, but I'll hold them till a later date. That's all for now.

Lots of love,

Dad

February 4, 1990

Dear Dad:

You're still stuck on the notion that humans are too small to be important in the total scheme of things. I suspect, Dad, that you're caught in the fairly common assumption that small = unimportant. It's frequently assumed that because we are so small in the physical scheme of things, we can't be important in the spiritual scheme of things.

But why should we assume this? Do we regard elephants as more important than human babies because they're bigger? Is Jupiter more important than Earth because it's 100 times larger? What's size got to do with anything?

If anything, it seems to me that God's personal characteristics are displayed all the more in our smallness. Just as we would admire a rich king who, for the sake of love, would be willing to forsake all for a peasant girl he fell in love with, so it seems that God's love for us is all the more magnified precisely because we are so small. The radical difference between a lover and the beloved displays the radical nature of the lover's love. In this light, God's love is shown to be "infinitely radical"! Maybe that's one reason why He made us so small in the physical scheme of things in the first place.

But I'd like to approach your position from a different angle. It strikes me that there's something inconsistent in your belief that God is personal, but not personally interested in us. You agree that our personal characteristics can only be explained if our Creator is personal, but then you suppose that our personal existence might just be an "accidental feature" to the Creator's overall agenda for the creation. But the whole force of positing a personal Creator to explain our personal characteristics in the first place is derived from the fact that our personal characteristics (our moral convictions, our reason, our love, etc.) could not come about by accident! Do you see the problem here?

Let me get at this by raising a set of different questions. Don't our imperfect personal characteristics presuppose the existence of a perfect personal being?

For example, don't our imperfect moral convictions presuppose the existence of a perfect moral standard? How else would we know ours is imperfect? And doesn't our imperfect reasoning and knowledge presuppose the existence of a perfect "reasoner" and "knower"? If the Creator is not perfectly moral and perfectly knowing, against what is His imperfection measured? I would argue that the Creator, by definition, is the definition of what it is to be perfect. For nothing, by definition, could be above him. (These are called the moral and epistemic arguments for God's existence. I deal with them in the book I'm working on which I sent you, Trinity and Process. But I'll spare you the details of them now. I promised before to stay as free from philosophy as possible.)

The gist of all this, Dad, is that if we imperfect beings are morally outraged at the injustices which exist in our world, must not the Creator be infinitely *more outraged? If we hurt, out of love and moral conviction, for those whom we know suffer in our world, must not the Creator hurt infinitely more? Would He not be less moral, less loving,*

71

LETTERS FROM A SKEPTIC

less knowing than us if this were not the case? But if this were the case, the effect (us) would be greater than the cause (God), and this is impossible.

The enormity of the cosmos, and our smallness in relation to it, would only present a problem for God's love and care if He were Himself one product of it (an effect). But He's behind the whole thing! His love and care is perfect, hence inexhaustible, and so whatever else He's got going in the universe (and for all I know He may have a lot!), there's plenty left over for us "small" human beings.

Thus I find it impossible to suppose that the ground of our personal characteristics (God) doesn't personally care about us.

The implications of this for our understanding of ourselves is, I think, enormous. It means, Dad, that God knows you — perfectly (better than you know yourself). It means that God loves you — perfectly (more than you love yourself). And it means that God cares about your suffering and moral convictions — perfectly (more than you care about them yourself).

It also means that it makes sense to begin inquiring about what relationship our Creator wants with us. What are His purposes for our lives? What does He want with us? What can we know about Him? Has He revealed Himself to us at any point? These questions follow naturally once we understand that God is already personally involved in our lives.

And this leads to one final point I want to make. I would maintain, Dad, that history shows to be true what reason says should be true. I would point to God's love and care for us not just by showing that reason demands it, but because history shows it. The answers to the questions raised above — e.g., where do we find out more about God? — are found in history in the person of Jesus Christ, and found in a way that confirms everything we already know about God through reason.

If God is the one perfect, loving, caring being, then we would suppose that He would do everything possible to bring about the greatest possible good for His creatures. Anything less would be less than perfect.

72

And Christ reveals that this is exactly what God did! God Himself became a man, one of us, and suffered a hellish death on the cross of Calvary in order to rectify all the evil which His personal creatures, humans, have inflicted on themselves. He has done, and is doing, everything possible ("possible" defined by the limits required by his overall agenda) to have us humans eternally with Him.

Not only does this fit reason. It also has a tremendous amount of historical evidence to support it. Reason and history come to the same end: Jesus Christ is Lord.

Let me know if you've followed my reasoning throughout this letter. I personally think it's pretty cogent (if I do say so myself), but I also know that parts of it may have been difficult to follow. And I want so much for you to grasp it!

Hope to hear from you soon. Let me again tell you how much I love our correspondence. When you finally convert (Am I confident or what?) our letters could be made into a book! Your questions are all the ones that need to be asked, and addressed, by believers and unbelievers alike.

With love, hope, and best wishes,

Greg

PART II
QUESTIONS
ABOUT
JESUS CHRIST

Why trust the Gospel accounts?

February 24, 1990

Dear Greg:

Your argument about God's perfection is very interesting. I've been thinking about it, and on one level it seems convincing, but then I come back to this question: is it really any deficiency in God if humans are just too insignificant to worry about? No one would think I'm less of a person for stepping on an ant, would they? Ants simply don't warrant that kind of consideration, though they are undoubtedly important in their own eyes. So also, in the total scheme of things it seems humans are less to God than ants are to us. It's not that He's defective: it's just that we don't amount to much.

But I have a more important problem with your last letter, especially the last part of it. This really gets to the heart of a lot of my problems with Christianity. Christians, especially the "born-again" types, are always quoting the Bible to back up their beliefs. They justify their beliefs as absolute truths because "the Bible tells me so." All I can say is, by whose authority is the Bible granted this lofty position?

So you say that "history" proves that God loves us, and then you quote the Bible! And I don't blame you because that's the only place you could ever find out anything about Jesus. But it just doesn't cut any mustard with me because I don't accept the Bible in the first place. I don't see any good reason to take the blind leap of faith to accept, lock, stock, and barrel the truthfulness of the Gospels your entire faith is based on.

So even if I were convinced that God cares about us ants, it's a long road to believing that He *became* one — and all that other Christian business.

Well, enough for now.

Lots of love,

Dad

March 8, 1990

Dear Dad:

Let me first address your ant analogy, and then turn to your objection about quoting the Bible.

You argued that just as a human is not less human because he doesn't care about ants, so God is not less God because He doesn't care about humans. I think your analogy is clever, but faulted.

It may lie outside the capacity of humans to care about bugs, but that's simply one more indication that we are imperfect. If we were perfectly loving, caring, sensitive, knowing, etc., we would care about bugs — and everything else in our world — and thus do everything possible to promote their good and minimize their suffering. We would empathize, not only with all other people, but with all other things.

This may sound corny, but let's start with the obvious and work toward the gray area. The imperfection of our love is clearly revealed in the inability, or just lack of willingness, of most people to care much about (say) the suffering of people we never see. It is further revealed in some people's inability to care about the welfare of "higher animals" — dogs, cats, monkeys. And it is even revealed in many people's inability to care about the plight of "lower animals" (e.g., those who for their own gain kill off species of animals by destroying forests, polluting water, etc.). So where can one draw the line where not caring any longer is seen as an imperfection? I don't think there is one.

78

Hence, if God treated us the way we treat ants, He wouldn't be a perfect being. But, for many reasons already given, I think it is established that God's existence is the standard of perfect love, knowledge, and moral conviction, and thus, I conclude, He does care about us (and ants).

*Now on to your more fundamental objection that I am assuming the authority of the Bible to prove that what the Bible says about Jesus is true. Dad, when I say that "history" shows what reason demands, I mean just that — history. Perhaps from your previous encounters with "born-again types" you assumed that I was just referring to the Bible as "God's Word" when I referred to Jesus being Lord, but I wasn't. It's true that almost all our knowledge about Jesus comes from the Gospels, but this doesn't mean that by referring to the Gospels I'm referring to them as God's Word. I'm not. I'm referring to them merely as histori-*cal documents.

Let me get at the difference between reading a document as "God's Word" and reading it as "history" this way. When your average Mormon reads the Book of Mormon, *he is reading it as God's Word. He accepts on faith that what the book says is true. When I read the* Book of Mormon, *however, I read it as history. I'm not Mormon. I use it only as a historical source. I apply to this work the same historical criteria any historian would use to evaluate any document of any possible historical value. I don't assume it is trustworthy at all. I invest only as much trust in it as the documents themselves warrant as shown by the degree to which they pass standard historical criteria. (In this light the* Book of Mormon *doesn't fare too well.)*

So it is with the Gospels, Dad. I'm not asking you to accept on "blind faith" that they are God's Word. Forget about that altogether for right now. I'm simply saying, look at them as you would any ancient document. Apply to them the same criteria historians apply to other ancient documents when they research history. And my contention is that, when the Gospels are treated in this critical-historical way, they fare very well and can be trusted to tell us a good deal about the person of Jesus Christ, enough, in fact, to know that God was present in Him and working through Him in a most significant way.

So what are the criteria which historians apply to ancient documents in order to ascertain their historical value? I'm not an expert in this area and, in any case, the field is far too vast to go into in any depth in our discussion. But most of these criteria are just common sense applied to historical documents. They can be divided into two groups: internal and external criteria. "Internal" criteria are criteria which apply inside the document under question. "External" criteria, obviously, are criteria which apply outside the document under consideration. You'll see the difference as I proceed. These criteria are best expressed by a series of questions which historians typically ask of ancient documents. Some of the more important ones, in both categories, follow (with a brief explanation of the rationale for each):

Internal Criteria
1. Was the author in a position to know what he or she is writing about? Does the text claim to be an eyewitness account, or based on an eyewitness account? Or is it based on hearsay?

If the document doesn't even claim to be an eyewitness account, or based on eyewitnesses, or at least written from an eyewitness perspective, its value is probably less than if it did make such a claim — though making the claim is not, of course, itself sufficient to prove the claim is true (see External Criteria).

2. Does the document in question contain specific, and especially irrelevant, material?

Firsthand sources are typically full of material, especially details, which aren't central to the story, whereas fabricated accounts tend to be generalized.

3. Does the document contain self-damaging material?

If a document includes material which could cast a negative image on the author, on the "heroes" of the story, or especially on the truthfulness of the story, this is typically a good indication that the author had truth as a central motive for writing.

80

4. Is the document reasonably self-consistent?

There is a coherence to truth which fabrications usually lack, though different perspectives on a single historical account usually include some minor discrepancies.

5. Is there evidence of legendary accretion in the document?

Fish stories tend to be exaggerated over time. The presence of "larger than life" features in a document suggest a later time of writing, and proportionally diminish the document's historical trustworthiness.

External Criteria:
1. Would the authors of the document have a motive for fabricating what they wrote?

Obviously, if a motive can be established for the author fabricating an account, the trustworthiness of the document is diminished. Conversely, if the author had nothing to gain, or even something to lose, by writing the account, the document's trustworthiness is increased.

2. Are there any other sources which confirm material in the document and/or which substantiate the genuineness of the document?

If a document's account can be, to any extent, confirmed by sources outside the document itself, this enhances the document's credibility (but the same criteria must be applied to these outside sources as well). And if the authorship of a document can be, to any extent, attested by outside sources, this enhances the document's credibility.

3. Does archeology support or go against material in the document?

If archeological findings can substantiate any material found in a document, the document's trustworthiness is increased. Conversely, if archeological findings stand in tension with the document, its credibility is damaged.

4. Could contemporaries of the document falsify the document's account, and would they have a motive for doing so?

If there existed persons who could have exposed the document's account as a fabrication, and had a motive for doing so, but nevertheless did not — so far as history tells — this increases the trustworthiness of the document.

Now the question, Dad, is this: how well do the Gospels fare when examined in the light of these criteria? And my claim is that they fare extremely well. I know this may be a bit tedious, but please follow with me as I briefly go through each one. This is important.

Internal #1

Luke, who is not an eyewitness, tells us that he is using eyewitness sources and that he is seeking to write an orderly and truthful account of the things he records (Luke 1:1-4). John tells us he is an eyewitness, and the other two Gospels, Mark and Matthew, are both written from the perspective of an eyewitness, though they don't come out and explicitly claim this: they just assume it. Other sources in the early second century confirm that the authors of the Gospels are Matthew, Mark, Luke, and John. (This is external criteria #2).

Internal #2

The Gospels are full of the sort of irrelevant detail which typically accompanies eyewitness accounts. Let me give you one example (which is all the more significant because it deals with the Resurrection). Read John 20:1-8 carefully. I've flagged for you the presence of irrelevant detail.

> Early on the first day of the week (when? does it matter?), while it was still dark (who cares?), Mary Magdalene (an incriminating detail, see the next criteria) went to the tomb and saw that the stone had been removed from the entrance. So she came running to Simon Peter and the other disciple, the one Jesus loved (John's modest way of referring to himself — another mark of genuineness) and said, "They have taken the Lord out of the tomb, and we don't know where they have put him!" (note her lack of faith here). So Peter and the other disciple started for the tomb. They were running, but the other disciple outran Peter and reached the tomb first (John's modesty again, but

who cares about this irrelevant detail?). *He bent over* (the tomb entrance was low — a detail which is historically accurate for tombs of wealthy people of the time — the kind we know Jesus was buried in) *and looked in at the strips of linen lying there but did not go in* (why not? irrelevant detail). *Then Simon Peter, who was behind him* (modest repetition again), *arrived and went into the tomb* (Peter's boldness stands out in all the Gospel accounts). *He saw the strips of linen lying there, as well as the burial cloth that had been around Jesus' head* (irrelevant and unexpected detail — what was Jesus wearing?). *The cloth was folded up by itself, separate from the linen* (could anything be more irrelevant, and more unusual, than this, Dad? Jesus folded one part of His wrapping before He left!). *Finally the other disciple, who reached the tomb first, also went inside* (who cares about what exact order they went in?).

I hope you get the point. There is absolutely no reason to throw in this sort of irrelevant detail. It contributes nothing to the story line, except it's just part of what happened, so the author throws it in as he is recalling the event. The Gospels are full of material like this.

Internal #3

The Gospels are also full of self-damaging detail. For example, in the Resurrection account you just read, a woman is said to be the first one to discover that the tomb was empty. But this could only damage the testimony of the early Christians, as women in first-century Jewish culture were regarded as incurable "talebearers." They couldn't even testify in court (which is why Paul doesn't include any women in his list of people who saw the risen Christ in 1 Cor. 15). Moreover, the disciples are consistently portrayed in a bad light. And even aspects of Jesus' life are included which, if the story were being fabricated to convince people of His messiahship, would have been excluded. For example, on the cross Jesus cried out "My God, My God, why have You forsaken Me?" Now this is hardly what one would expect from the Messiah, especially if the Messiah is supposed to be divine. It's a tough statement, but that just proves the point. The only motive anyone could have for including it in his account is because Jesus actually said it!

Internal #4

The Gospels present a consistent portrait of who Jesus is and what He did, as well as of the events which surrounded His life. If the four accounts were individually fabricated, where did this consistency come from? But there are also significant differences in each account, showing the relative differences of their perspectives. If they were all fabricated together, the consistency would be greater than we find.

Internal #5

C.S. Lewis was a professor at Oxford and an expert on ancient mythology. He once said, "as a literary historian, I am perfectly convinced that whatever else the Gospels are they are not legends. I have read a great deal of legend, and I am quite clear that they are not the same sort of things."[1] The Gospels do include supernatural acts, but the accounts which we find in the Gospels don't have any of the features of ancient mythology. They are very sober.

Now let's turn to the external criteria.

External #1

What possible motive would the early disciples have had for fabricating stories about Jesus? They claimed to believe in Jesus because of His miracles and His resurrection, combined with the kind of life He lived and teachings He gave. And far from gaining anything from this, they suffered great persecution for it. Why would they lie? And is there anything about their characters which would lead us to think that they were the kind of people who deceived others? No scholar I know of doubts the disciples' sincerity.

External #2

As I said before, the authorship of these Gospels is attested to by numerous sources in the second century, and they were in a better position to know than anyone is today. We can also ascertain some things about Jesus and the early disciples, things which fit in well with the Gospels, from other secular ancient sources such as Tacitus (ca. 55-120), Suetonius (early second century), Josephus (ca. 37-97), Thallus (mid first century), Pliny (early second century), as well as ancient Jewish writings written against the Christians (the Talmud).

External #3
While there have always been archeologists who claim that their findings are in tension with some aspect of the biblical account of things, time and time again these findings have been reversed in favor of the biblical account. To give one example, it used to be held by some that Luke's account of the birth of Jesus was fabricated. He says that an empire-wide census was being taken during the reign of Caesar Augustus, when Quirinius was governor of Syria. Mary and Joseph had to go to Bethlehem where Joseph was born to register, which is when Jesus was born. But we know from other ancient sources (e.g., Josephus) that Quirinius was governor beginning in A.D. 6, and there was no evidence for a census like this ever being taken. So, it was assumed, Luke must be in error. We now know, however, that censuses like the kind Luke mentioned were frequent, and Quirinius' reign in A.D. 6 was his second reign. I know of no conclusive archeological finding which refutes conclusively any biblical account, but I do know of many conclusive archeological findings which substantiate the biblical account — often after the biblical account has been accused of error on the basis of a previously misinterpreted finding.

External #4
Finally, Christianity was born in a very hostile environment. There were contemporaries who would have refuted the Gospel portrait of Jesus — if they could have. The leaders of Judaism in the first century tended to view Christianity as a pernicious cult and would have loved to see it stamped out. And this would have been easy to do — if the "cult" had been based on fabrications. Why, just bringing forth the body of the slain Jesus would have been sufficient to extinguish Christianity once and for all.

In spite of this, however, Christianity exploded (in a positive sense). The disciples preached their Gospel to people who had been eyewitnesses of the things they claimed Jesus said and did. How could they have *fabricated it? And even those who remained opposed to Christianity did not deny that Jesus did miracles, and did not deny that His tomb was empty. The* facts *behind the Gospel are not questioned. What is questioned is how the facts were established. The opponents claimed that Jesus did what He did either through trickery, or the power of Satan, and that the disciples stole the body of Jesus (but see External criteria #1).*

So to sum it all up, Dad, I think we have very good grounds for treating the Gospels like generally reliable documents. They are generally good sources of history for us. And this has nothing to do with them being "inspired" or "God's Word": it is just history.

In the face of this history, one must make a decision. One must regard Jesus as being either a demonic charlatan tricking His way into people's faith (and getting crucified for it), or as the Lord which He and His followers claimed He was. My claim is that only the latter conclusion is founded on the evidence.

Well, I apologize for this being such a long letter. But the issues had to be addressed. Chew on it a while and let me know what you think. OK?

With sincere love and hope,

Greg

––––––––––

¹C.S. Lewis, *God in the Dock* (Grand Rapids: Eerdmans Publishing Company, 1970), p. 158.

CORRESPONDENCE 14

Aren't the Gospels full of contradictions?

April 14, 1990

Dear Greg:

Sorry it's taken me a while to get back to you, but your last letter took some time to digest. How are you and the family doing these days? Are you planning on doing any of your crazy ultramarathons this year? How are the girls coming along in gymnastics, running, choir, and the other 600 things they're involved in?

Well, your last letter sort of threw me for a loop. As you suspected, I was assuming that you were just taking it for granted that what the Bible said was fact, and then arguing with me on this basis. But then you threw all this "criteria" business at me. This isn't the way born-again types are supposed to use the Bible!

I read your letter several times and have been giving it a lot of thought. Here are some of my reflections.

First, I don't see how anyone can base their faith on how well a certain document meets historical criteria because all of it is guess work, nothing is certain. But isn't your faith something you're certain of? Most of the Christians I've ever run into are so certain that they're right—on every point—that there's little sense in discussing anything with them.

Secondly, you did a good "sell job" on the Gospels but, having been a salesman myself, I don't believe this is the whole story. Now, I'm no Bible scholar, but I've read that a lot of Bible scholars who aren't fundamentalist don't think the Gospels have much historical value. I read in *Time* that there's a committee of New Testament scholars who get together every year and vote on whether the sayings attributed to Jesus in the Gospels are really *His!* We don't even know what He actually taught, but you're trying to tell me to trust these writings to tell me He's the Almighty here on earth!

Along these same lines, I've read somewhere or other that a lot of scholars believe that the Gospels, and most of the rest of the Bible, are pieced together from previous sources. Doesn't this go against any theory of the whole Bible being "divinely inspired"? It's also said that the Gospels are full of contradictions, that the order of the events in each is arranged all differently, that the teachings of Jesus are found in different contexts, and the like. In my mind this undermines their historical reliability.

Finally, even if these Gospels are accurate at points — they pass your historical tests — this doesn't mean that they are completely accurate. If they were pieced together from previous sources like the liberal scholars say, maybe some of these earlier sources are accurate here and there, but mixed in with this are all sorts of tall tales and legends about the man they're writing about. "Fish stories" get bigger and bigger, but there's always an element of truth passed on along the way.

So the whole enterprise of proving the Gospels to be true seems too "iffy" to me. It's nothing I'd want to stake my life on.

Give my love to Shelley and the kids. Hope to hear from you soon.

Love always,

Dad

April 26, 1990

Dear Dad:

Good to hear from you again. The family here is all doing well. The girls are very involved in gymnastics and, if I may say so, are getting very good at it. They don't express much interest in running these days, so I pretty much go to the races alone. I haven't had time to train much, but if I can get my mileage up, I'd like to compete in the 100 kilometer World Championship this year. It is being held in the United States for the first time in history, and it will be held right here in Minnesota! It's an opportunity I'd not like to miss.

Now on to your letter. I hope you have a copy of it because I'd like to address your points one by one.

First, you asked about the relationship between my faith and all of this discussion on the credibility of the Gospels. My faith doesn't hang on the demonstrable credibility of these documents in every detail, but it does hang on their overall credibility. The Jesus I am personally related to can't be wholly different from the Jesus of history as shown by these documents, otherwise "my Jesus" isn't the Jesus I think He is. The certainty I have on the truth of my faith thus attaches both to my experience of Christ in worship and to my investigation of the Gospel accounts which, to my mind at least, has shown them to be at least generally reliable. Faith is a loving, trusting relationship with Christ, an attachment which goes way beyond a theoretical assessment of ancient documents. But it isn't divorced from this historical assessment. It's much like our relationships with others. Your relationship with Jeanne, for example, goes way beyond the factual information you know about her, but you'd have a hard time being related to her in the first place without this information.

Secondly, you raised questions about the construction and consistency of the Gospels, and whether or not we can even know for sure what Jesus said. It is true that most scholars believe that the Gospels utilized sources, oral and written, when they composed their accounts. I completely accept this. The evidence for it is irrefutable. But I don't see anything radical or "liberal" about this. Luke, after all, tells us himself that he is utilizing the sources available to him (Luke 1:1-4). Neither do I see how this diminishes the authors' credibility in the least. In fact, in my view it enhances their credibility in that it ties them in with pre-existent material which brings us even closer to the original events they are talking about. Whenever they actually composed their Gospels (probably between A.D. 50 to 70), the evidence clearly demonstrates that they to some extent utilized material which was circulating for some time before this date. And the closer the material of a document is to the events of which it speaks, the more solid is its claim to report those events accurately.

It is also true that the order of events in all the Gospels varies a great deal, but I again don't see this as diminishing their credibility. Dad, the Gospels are not trying, on every point, to just give us biographical information on the life of Jesus. They were not written to satisfy historical curiosity. They were written to save people by bringing them into a relationship with the Savior. They are each painting a portrait of the historical Christ — an "impressionistic painting" if you will — and thus they rearrange material to fit the theme of their portrait. Like a well-constructed sermon, they tell their story with an eye both on the history of what happened and on how their telling of the story will impact their audience. Or to use a different analogy, the Gospels are like a song which communicates information in its lyrics, but does so in such a way that more than cognitive communication takes place: the heart is moved and transformed as well.

None of this, I argue, diminishes the Gospels' general reliability. All the historical works of this time period were written in just the same fashion. It only means we can't know for sure the exact order in which the events of Jesus' life took place (though a general order is certainly discernable). But what difference could this information make?

The same may be said of the words of Jesus. The Gospels vary a good deal on what exactly Jesus said, and when exactly He said it. But this just shows that the writers were not 20th-century people concerned with the exact wording of things. They paraphrase Jesus in their own words to bring out the meaning which they feel their audience needs to hear. This simply shows how rich the teachings of Jesus were. The Gospels do what no "snapshot-tape recording" account of Jesus could ever do: they bring out the theological and personal significance of His life and teachings for readers. They can only be faulted for doing this if they were themselves trying to adhere to a 20th-century "snapshot-tape recording" criteria of literal accuracy.

As far as I'm concerned, the attempt of scholars to arrive at the exact words of Jesus — by a vote? — is as futile as it is needless. I regard the effort of fundamentalists to get everything in the Gospels to "harmonize" perfectly in exactly the same fashion.

This is also how I'd address your charge that the Gospels are "full of contradictions." Almost all of the alleged "contradictions" in the Gospels are the result of people misusing the Gospels, viz., treating them like 20th-century works which work under a "snapshot-tape recording" criteria of truth. But if they are read in accordance with their first-century context and the purpose for which they are written, the "contradictions" disappear. Not because they are explained away, but because they instantly become totally irrelevant.

So, Dad, I stand by my claim that the Gospels are trustworthy. There's a lot they don't tell us which, perhaps, our historical curiosity would like to know. But they nevertheless tell us all that we need to know and thus force us to answer an all-important question: who was Jesus Christ? And with this question comes a decision: was He a lunatic, was He a liar, or was He the Lord His followers proclaimed Him to be? The evidence which addresses the mind, and the Spirit of God which addresses the heart, both point to the last of these alternatives as the only possible answer.

Think about it, Dad.

Whether you like it or not, you should know that I'm praying a lot for you.

Because I love you,

Greg

CORRESPONDENCE 15

Who wrote the Gospels, and when?

May 3, 1990

Dear Greg:

Good to hear that all is going well with all of you. Please keep me up to date on your racing schedule. I'm especially interested, and worried, about your plans to compete in the 100k championships. Running that far can't be good for anyone. And how you find it to be "fun" is way beyond me. That comes close to being as good a definition of hell as I can think of.

So our debate continues. I've got to tell you that I feel way over my head in all of this. I felt a little more in the ballpark talking about God, but this historical stuff is too much. I just can't get used to looking at any part of the Bible in this "historical" fashion. I'm surprised to hear you conceding that the Gospels have all these differences, that they used previous sources, etc. I always thought you evangelical types saw this "Holy Book" as sort of dropping out of heaven, perfect in every detail, "inerrant" like the Southern Baptists say. Don't you believe that?

In any case, I see the case you're trying to make, and I find it very interesting. But here's my objection for the day: how can you be sure when these books were written, and how can you even be sure who wrote them? In fact, given the fact that they've been passed down to us hand by hand for so long, how can you even be sure you have the original Gospels? Maybe they've been "doctored up" along the way.

I suspect you've got an answer for this. Let me know what it is.

Lots of love,

Dad

May 23, 1990

Greetings once again dearest Father:

Yes, the debate goes on! I'll jump right in.

You inquired how I can believe the Bible to be inspired and yet treat it in the historical fashion I'm treating it. I agree with you, Dad, that most evangelicals treat the Bible as though it fell from heaven, but I think this is a mistaken conception and has nothing to do with inspiration. Though I believe the Bible is inspired, and even infallible, it also clearly is a collection of books written by humans in the same fashion other books are written. When I say that the Bible is "inspired," I'm expressing my conviction that God worked through — not above — the historical process which brought the Bible into being. I thus don't see any incompatibility in believing the Bible is God's Word and also analyzing it in the same historical fashion I'd analyze any other work of history.

I have many reasons for believing the Bible is inspired, and at some point we'll need to talk about that. But believing the Bible to be inspired is, in my mind, not as central to what Christianity is about as is believing that Jesus Christ was God Incarnate and can be the Lord and Savior of your life. Salvation is a matter of being related to Christ, not the Bible. In fact, believing the Bible to be inspired is, for me, simply a consequence (not the basis) of confessing Christ to be the Lord of my life.

Let me turn, then, to your question about the dating and authorship of the Gospels. Like the issue of testing the reliability of ancient documents, this can also be a complex and tedious issue. But I'll strive to keep it simple and brief.

First of all, let me say that nothing centrally important to Christianity hangs on how well the early date and the apostolic authorship of the Gospels can be defended. That is, even if the Gospels were composed by

93

persons other than the disciples to whom they are ascribed, at a date later than they are traditionally regarded as being written, their overall credibility can nevertheless be demonstrated on numerous other grounds (some of which I gave you in a previous letter). So even if it could be conclusively proven that the Gospels were written at the very end of the first century by unknown persons, I would still regard their portrait of Jesus as being accurate enough to tell me this: there was a Jewish man in the early first century who made divine claims for Himself and whose life, teachings, and miraculous deeds — including a resurrection from the dead — were able to convince orthodox Jews (whose entire belief system went against any human claims to divinity) that His claims were true. I would still be forced into the position of having to decide whether this first-century Rabbi named Jesus was an unthinkably clever charlatan (but very stupid as well, for He got Himself crucified), or whether He was speaking the truth. There is just too much evidence substantiating the general reliability of these documents to brush the traditional portrait of Jesus aside, even if a late date for the Gospels were accepted. If they themselves are late, much of the material they contain certainly is not.

Nevertheless, if an early date and apostolic authorship of the Gospels can be demonstrated, so much the better. And this, I believe, can be demonstrated with reasonable certainty. The key to dating the Gospels, Dad, is in dating the Book of Acts, for it is accepted by almost all scholars (liberal and conservative) that Acts comes after the Gospels (with the possible exception of John). The synoptic Gospels, then, cannot be dated later than Acts. So what is the dating of Acts? I would argue that it must be dated some time in the early 60s of the first century. Here are my reasons.

1. Luke (the accepted author of Acts) makes no mention of the fall of Jerusalem in A.D. 70. This would be most remarkable if Acts was written after this date, especially because Luke is, throughout Acts, centrally interested in events which occur in Jerusalem. In fact, Dad, Luke makes no mention of the war that broke out between the Jews and the Romans in A.D. 66 which led to the fall of Jerusalem, though throughout his work he is concerned with Roman-Jewish relations. For example, he mentions the minor skirmish which occurred between these two in A.D. 44. But how could he then pass up the much more significant war which occurred 22 years later, a war which resulted in the destruction of the Jewish temple and the sacking of all Jerusalem?

What really drives home this point is the fact that Jesus, in Luke's Gospel, prophesies that Jerusalem would fall (Luke 21). It is, I think, most unlikely to suppose that Luke missed this opportunity to show how this prophecy was fulfilled — especially when one considers that one of the reasons Luke wrote Acts in the first place was to show how the working of the Spirit in the early church carries on and fulfills the ministry of Jesus!

In fact, all the Gospels record Jesus prophesying the destruction of Jerusalem. Now, liberal scholars who don't believe anything supernatural can occur, argue that this shows that the Gospels must be written after the fall of Jerusalem (a main reason they date the Gospels late). The Gospel authors thus supposedly put into Jesus' mouth a prophecy He never made. But what's interesting to observe here is that in all the Gospels the fall of Jerusalem is connected closely with the end of the world (Luke 21; Matt. 24; Mark 13). This raises problems for interpreters because, obviously, the world didn't end when Jerusalem fell (don't worry, there is an answer to that). But the problem in the text raises an even more serious problem for the liberal view. For if the Gospel authors were fabricating a prophecy of Jesus about Jerusalem after the fact, they certainly wouldn't have fabricated a connection between it and something they knew did not occur, namely, the end of the world! Do you see the point?

So I conclude that the prophecy of Jesus concerning the fall of Jerusalem in A.D. 70 had to have been written prior to A.D. 70. Luke would have mentioned it being fulfilled in Acts, and none of the authors would have connected it with the world ending if, in fact, it had been written (fabricated) after this date.

2. *Acts makes no mention of Nero's persecution of Christians in the mid-60s. In fact, his view of the Roman government is positively irenic. This requires us to place the document at a time when the Roman government was not hostile to Christians, a time prior to Nero.*

3. Luke, in Acts, makes no mention of the martyrdom of Paul (A.D. 64) and Peter (A.D. 65), though he is very concerned to note the martyrdoms of "lesser" Christian leaders (e.g., Stephen, James). This is especially remarkable because half the Book of Acts is about Paul, and a large part is about Peter! This is impossible to make sense of if Luke were writing after their deaths.

4. Much of the subject matter of Acts concerns issues which are important before the fall of Jerusalem, but not after. This reflects the needs and interests of the audience, an audience which clearly has not yet experienced the fall of Jerusalem.

5. Luke's record of people and events in the Roman Empire has time and time again been substantiated by archeology. He reflects a detailed knowledge of the early first century, a knowledge which grows increasingly unlikely the later we place the date of this document.

6. Luke uses expressions in Acts which were used widely early on in Christianity, but not later — not after A.D. 70. Jesus, for example, is called "the Son of Man," but this title of Jesus died out very early in Christian circles (replaced by "Son of God").

So, I would argue, Acts can be dated no later than the mid-60s, and probably a bit earlier. The Gospel of Luke was written just prior to Acts — they form a two-volume work — and Luke, it is almost universally argued, was written after Mark. It is also usually argued, for a number of good reasons, that Matthew and Luke are roughly contemporaneous with each other. One reason for this assumption is that they both utilized Mark, in roughly the same form, and both utilized another source (called "Q") in roughly the same form. So the dating of these three Gospels (called "the Synoptic Gospels") must be sometime prior to the mid-60s.

The implications of this, Dad, are significant. Here we have documents which were written no later than three decades after the event. That is very close, by any historical standards. There was no time for significant "legendary" accretion. The eyewitnesses, especially those hostile to the Gospel message, were still living, and living in the very same vicinity as *where these works were being circulated. (The Gospels thus have a built-in "reality check.") And much of the material which is incorporated into the Gospels goes back even further in proximity to the events being recorded.*

All of this, combined with the evidence of reliability I presented to you earlier, requires that we view the Gospels as being at least generally trustworthy documents.

Now on the issue of the Gospels' authorship, let me just make three brief points. First, the authorship of the Gospel of Luke and Acts is not much disputed. It is, as the documents themselves say, and as early sources confirm, Luke. The case for the Christian view of Christ could stand on this alone.

Secondly, the authorship of the other three Gospels is confirmed early in the second century by people who were in a position to know. These people would want to know because they were, at this time, being persecuted, and even martyred, for their faith. And no one wants to die for a lie.

Third, this early tradition fits with almost everything else we know about these Gospels: they everywhere reflect the perspectives of people close to the events they record. To add one more thing to the evidence I've already given you, one finds throughout the Synoptic Gospels (John paraphrases much more) a recognizable "style" to Jesus' teaching. Though they reword His teachings to an extent, His unique way of teaching comes out in all three. For example, He often uses a threefold pattern to His teaching. He uses "amen" (= truly) in a very unique way. He raises questions in a distinct manner, etc. If the authors were not associated with Jesus, and if they were fabricating this (why would they want to do that?), this commonality between the authors would be inexplicable.

Now I grant that none of this constitutes absolute certainty. But if anyone is going to deny this authorship, the burden of proof clearly lies on them to show why these early traditions are inaccurate, and how these documents mistakenly came to be ascribed to these authors in the first place. And this no one has done, at least not to my satisfaction.

My case, then, stands like this, Dad. We have in our hands documents which show, with reasonable accuracy, a person who made divine claims for Himself and who substantiated these claims forcefully enough to completely overturn the theology of His Jewish audience. He convinced them that He was in fact the Lord on earth, the Messiah, the Savior of the world — no small feat! And the way He did this, we see in the Gospels and in the Epistles, was by living a life and performing deeds which no ordinary man could do. Especially His miracles, and His resurrection, convinced His followers-to-be that He could only be "the Son of God."

The question which these documents confront us with is, Who do we say Jesus is? If not who He and His followers said, then what?

Dad, you and I have gotten to the point in our discussion where we've agreed that God does exist, and that He is a personal being who knows, loves, and cares about us more than we could care ourselves. So the question I pose to you is this: doesn't this testimony of the Gospels "fit"? Doesn't the proclamation that "in Christ God was redeeming the world" (2 Cor. 5:19, my paraphrase) not only square with the historical evidence, but square with this view of God as well? Doesn't this proclamation confirm the longings of the heart in the same fashion it answers the questions of the mind? I hope you think about it, and (who knows?) maybe even pray about it.

Sorry to be so long-winded, but it's your own fault for asking such good questions. If you'd just convert, we wouldn't have to go into all this! Just kidding. I actually love it — which is why I'm making a living thinking about these sorts of things. I'm only concerned I'm taxing your patience a bit by being too technical. Forgive me. But I frankly don't know how else to adequately address the questions you're raising.

I look forward to hearing from you.

With love and hope,

Greg

How can you believe that a man rose from the dead?

May 29, 1990

Dear Greg:

I find your approach to Jesus and the Bible to be as odd as I found your view of God to be. You say that your belief in the Bible comes *after* your belief in Jesus? This is reversed from what I've always assumed — but I see what you're getting at. And then there's your understanding of inspiration. It's completely foreign to what I've always heard. Do other people at Bethel think that way? Or are you an off-the-wall liberal among fundamentalists?

In any case, Greg, you've pretty much convinced me that the Gospels have a good bit of reliable, firsthand material. I'm impressed with your case. But you haven't proven that these works are reliable *in every respect* (and you didn't show how the Gospel of John is reliable in *any* respect). And so the point I have to make in response to your arguments is one I've raised before. What's to prevent us from supposing that there are a good many "tall tales" spun into the historical material of the Gospels, just like there are "tall tales" spun throughout the whole Bible?

I'm not denying the Gospels' "general reliability," and I'm not denying that Jesus perhaps did some kind of "faith healing" of some sort — that's seen in other religions too — but then maybe the stories just grew and grew, till by the time the Gospels were written, He was believed to be the Savior of the world! Isn't this what always happens to remarkable people? People tell miracle stories about Buddha and Muhammad too, you know.

At the heart of this question is a fundamental problem I have with the whole Christian business. Every dead person I've ever known has stayed dead! But Christians say that Jesus rose from the dead. You're asking me to overturn all this evidence I (and everyone else who has ever lived) have that people stay dead because of the "general reliability" of some ancient documents I don't know much about. Would you believe a "generally reliable" person today if they told you a friend of theirs walked out of his own tomb?

I don't know why the disciples *thought* Jesus rose from the dead, but it seems to me that *any* explanation is better than the one which assumes that He actually *did* rise from the dead. Maybe the disciples hallucinated. That happened at Fatima, and I've heard of it happening in other places. People see weird things, especially religious fanatics. Look at Oral Roberts! Or maybe someone stole the body, maybe some pranksters. Or maybe Jesus contrived the whole thing somehow. That's what Schonfield says in *The Passover Plot*. I really don't know. But I sure as hell don't buy the story that He just appears after death with all those angels and things.

Well, you asked me at the end of your last letter who I thought Jesus was. It's a question I frankly don't have a definite answer for. But one thing I am quite sure of. Whoever He was, He isn't that *now* — He's dead.

We may have hit a stalemate here, Greg, because I think that what I'm objecting to here is simply an article of faith, and faith is the one thing I lack. You either believe this or you don't. It goes beyond the "general reliability" of any ancient documents.

You've got to be getting tired of me by now! We've been going at this for over a year, and despite all your intellectual arguments which I greatly admire, I don't think I'm much closer to accepting your faith than I was before. My view of God has, to some extent, changed, but otherwise I'm just a lot more informed.

Be that as it may, I love you.

Dad

June 16, 1990

Dear Dad:

I trust all is going well for you down there in inferno land. You may mock us during our frigid winters, but the joke's on you during the summer. I see the kind of heat you've been having. I bet you go outdoors less in the summer than we do in the winter! Ah, truly this is a fallen universe. There's no Garden of Eden where there isn't some season or another to torment our poor souls.

OK, let's talk theology. I've set aside the entire afternoon for this letter because I think it's going to be my magnum opus *to you. I want to talk about the Resurrection, and this is, I believe, perhaps the single most critical issue to be discussed between us.*

Let me first respond to your concern that I'm growing tired of your skepticism. Perish the thought! I admire the strength of your character and the astuteness of your questions and objections. I'm loving this! Beyond my love for the subject, I'm just enjoying dialoguing with you about the most important things in life. We've never talked like this before.

But I also know something you don't — and this also fuels my fire. You see, Dad, you are a marked man. God's got your number! He's passionately in love with you and wants you with Him throughout eternity. And in spite of all the issues with His program which you have in your mind, He knows that your heart is pliable. My job is simply to get the intellectual issues cleared up as much as possible so He can have free access to your heart. I think He's getting that, more and more with each letter.

This confidence, combined with my love and concern for you, inspires me on. Call it gut instinct, but I just have this fundamental conviction that you are going to be saved. You probably aren't aware of it, and maybe there's little evidence of it yet. But when I pray for you, there's a confidence that comes over me. It's the Spirit of God, the same Spirit which is chipping away at your skeptical heart. This no doubt sounds corny to you, but that doesn't bother me. I'm convinced you'll look back on this someday and see it as well. In any case, you don't need to worry about fatigue from my end of the conversation.

OK, let's turn to your objections about the Resurrection.

First, you hold that the Resurrection is simply "an article of faith" that one simply believes or doesn't. So you suspect we've hit a stalemate. I don't agree. Of course a belief in the Resurrection is more than a theoretical hypothesis about a historical event, but this doesn't mean that it has nothing to do with a hypothesis about a historical event. The event took place in history, and thus it must be ascertained by historical criteria, just like any other supposed historical event. It takes more than evidence to believe in the Resurrection of Christ — I believe it also takes the Spirit of God working in a person's heart — but this doesn't mean that this belief can or should be held apart from historical evidence. When it comes to truth, the mind and the Spirit work in harmony.

Now I can't worry about the Spirit's job to convict your heart (I'm not the Holy Spirit!), but I sure as heck can concern myself with the business of convincing your mind. So I'd like to talk with you about the evidence for the Resurrection. It isn't simply "an article of faith." It's an article of faith that intersects with historical reasoning.

Secondly, you rightly pointed out that while I demonstrated the "general reliability" of the Gospels (excluding John, but that's another very involved story on which nothing hangs), I did not prove that the Gospels are trustworthy "in every respect." But is this a reasonable demand, Dad? How could one ever prove such a thing about any ancient historical document? I've been maintaining that we must treat the Gospels just like we treat other ancient documents, but what you're asking for goes way beyond this.

It is, of course, possible that there are aspects of the Gospels which are not reliable, but the thrust of showing that the Gospels are generally reliable is that the burden of proof is now on the person who denies the Gospels' reliability in a certain respect to show why they should be so regarded. If there are "tall tales" in the Gospels, this must be proven, for we have good grounds for holding them to be trustworthy.

Related to this is my third point. You suspect that legendary features have crept into the historical core of the Gospels. But on what grounds do you hold this? From all I've been able to find (and I study this material a good deal), the only real basis anyone has for making this claim is that there are supernatural aspects to Jesus' life in the Gospels and supernatural events. Hence the Gospel accounts are, to this extent, legendary.

But from where do such people get their infallible knowledge about the universe? The notion that we live in a universe where every event must have a natural cause is as much a matter of "blind faith" as anything could be! What is more, it seems to be a notion which isn't available to you, because you already believe that there is a personal God behind, or above, the universe. And if there is such a deity, how can we rule out the possibility of His intervention? To the contrary, if He is the supreme example of everything we are, I would think we would expect such intervention.

There are also four historical arguments against the theory that the Gospels contain legendary material. First, the Gospels are written within several decades of the events they record, and that is not enough time for significant legendary accretion to occur. Second, the Gospels are written in a hostile environment which would necessarily hold in check the development of legendary accretion.

Third, if legendary accretion did occur, we would expect to find it in the later strata of the Gospel material, but not in the earlier. Many liberal theologians in the eighteenth and nineteenth centuries tried to prove this. But the whole thing collapsed because it couldn't be done. The earliest material is just as filled with miracles as the later. In fact, the Epistles of Paul represent a fully "divinized" view of Jesus (viz., He is Lord and God), and most of them are, by all accounts, written before any of the Gospels (and even these letters contain material which can be

*proven to predate their composition, material which has a fully super-
natural Jesus! i.e., Phil. 2:6-11). No, the supernatural features of Jesus'
life did not develop over time. They were there from the start!*

*Finally, if the Gospels contained legendary material amidst their other-
wise trustworthy material, we should expect this material would not
pass our earlier discussed "historical criteria" as well as their other
"non-legendary" material. But this is simply not the case. Recall the
Resurrection narrative of John 20 which I shared with you. It has all
the characteristics of an eyewitness report.*

*Hence, Dad, I see no good reason to reverse our assessment of the
general reliability of the Gospels when it comes to their narratives about
supernatural events. And this applies also to their Resurrection accounts. If someone is going to deny the reliability of these accounts,
then the burden of proof is on him to say why. But this, I think, is very
difficult to do. As a matter of fact, the evidence for the historicity of the
Resurrection is, in my estimation, stronger than for any other event of
Jesus' life — and stronger than the evidence for the historicity of many
other historical events we take for granted. Let me briefly lay out my
case for you.*

*1. The Resurrection event is testified to by five independent sources
(Matthew, Mark, Luke, John, and Paul — who refer to numerous other
sources as well, such as Peter and James in 1 Cor. 15). This plurality of
sources greatly enhances the credibility of each. One might hold that
Matthew and Luke borrowed from Mark here as they did in some of
their other material. But what's interesting is that their individual narratives of the Resurrection completely differ from Mark and from each other!
In fact, each of the testimonies has more unique material than it has
material in common with the others. This creates a problem with harmo-
nizing the accounts. But that problem is nothing compared to the
problem of explaining how each independently testifies to the Resurrection in the first place — if, in fact, the Resurrection never occurred.*

*2. The location of Jesus' tomb was well known by all, so if Jesus had
not risen from the dead, if His body were yet in the tomb, this could*

have been easily checked out. Both Jesus' followers (who would suffer persecution for their faith) and the opponents of Jesus (who would want to falsify the Christian claim) would have a motive for checking this out. But all agreed, the tomb was empty. How is this agreement to be explained?

3. *Related to #2, no one disputes that the Christian church began in Jerusalem just a few weeks after Jesus' crucifixion. It exploded in growth. And the content of the message that caused this explosion was that Jesus was the Messiah, the Lord of all, as was evidenced by His miracles and resurrection from the dead (see Acts 2:16ff). They do not present to their audience some unknown figure in the distant past. They're talking about one of their audience's contemporaries! How is this growth to be explained?*

4. *As I stated earlier, the Resurrection narratives lack the characteristics common to late legendary narratives, and embody many of the characteristics common to early eyewitness-based reports. There is, for example, much detail, much of it being irrelevant to the story line. To give one illustration, Mark mentions the name of the well-known member of the Sanhedrin (a Jewish councilman) who donated a tomb for Jesus — Joseph of Arimathea. Now if one is going to fabricate an account, one doesn't create this sort of detail. One certainly doesn't drop names of such prominent people, people who can easily be cross-examined.*

There is also a good bit of counter-productive material. Legends lack this. The role of women in the story, for example, could, in the first century context, do nothing but damage the testimony of the authors. They were, as I said in an earlier letter, regarded as being incurable liars.

And, finally, there is a total lack of theological reflection in the narratives. Later legendary material leaves nothing unexplained, but the Gospel narratives contain many puzzling features which the authors simply report, but leave puzzling. For example, Jesus tells Mary Magdalene in John 20: "Do not hold on to Me, for I have not yet returned to the Father." Why not? The author doesn't say. Theologians today are still guessing at the explanation. Numerous other examples could be given.

5. *The conversion of Paul is unexplainable except on the basis he himself gives: he confronted the risen Lord (see Acts 9 and 1 Cor. 15). Here was a man dead set against Christianity, even overseeing the stoning of one of its preachers, and then in one moment he's converted. Similarly, James, the brother of Jesus, was also a nonbeliever in Jesus until the Lord appeared to him (1 Cor. 15:7). (We find this unbelief referred to in Mark 3 and John 7 — more counter-productive material substantiating their reliability!) What explains this conversion if not the actual Resurrection?*

6. *Paul gives us an early list of the Resurrection appearances. It's found in 1 Corinthians 15, written about 15 to 20 years after the Resurrection. He is here attempting to convince some Corinthians that the Resurrection of Jesus did in fact occur, and to do this he lists Christ's appearance to the apostles, and to James, and "to more than 500 at the same time, most of whom are still living" (1 Cor. 15:6). The thrust of noting the large number of living people who saw Christ resurrected is to say "if you don't believe me, the evidence is still around. Go and ask those who saw it." By the standards of any law court, this must be taken as strong evidence.*

7. *There is no way of accounting for the transformation of the disciples except on the basis of the Resurrection, the very basis they themselves give. If you compare the disciples before the death of Jesus with the disciples after the Resurrection appearances, you will see a world of difference. One day they are fearful and hiding; the next day they are facing hostile audiences preaching (what else?) the Resurrection.*

8. *Finally, there is no motive for the disciples to fabricate this story. They had nothing to gain and everything to lose. Nor is there anything to lead us to believe that they were disposed to fabricate such a story, or had the sort of characters which would be capable of such an incredible* *fabrication. Nor is there anything to suggest that they could have successfully pulled such an incredible fabrication off, even if they had wanted to.*

In short, the denial of the Resurrection has nothing to recommend itself as a historical hypothesis, while the admittance of the Resurrection has everything to recommend itself as a historical hypothesis. Such, in a nutshell, is my historical case for the Resurrection.

Now I'd like to conclude my magnum opus *with a few words about the alternative explanations for the Resurrection which you voiced in your last letter.*

Could someone have stolen the body? Who could this be? Who would have had an interest in doing this? How could they have gotten past the Roman guards (whose lives could be at stake in protecting it)? And how does this explain the Resurrection appearances?

Could the disciples have just hallucinated about "seeing" Jesus? How does this explain the empty tomb? And besides, the appearances have none of the qualities of hallucinations. They occur over a relatively long period of time. They occurred to groups of people at the same time (who interact with, even eat with, the "hallucination"). The disciples were not predisposed to having such a hallucination. And the appearances transformed those who witnessed them. Hallucinations don't have this effect.

Could Jesus have contrived the whole thing? How could He have pulled this off? How does one contrive a death (amidst executioners who are experts of death) and a resurrection? Is this consistent with anything else we know about the character of Jesus and the disciples? How does this explain the appearances to Paul, James, and the 500? How does this explain the disciples' transformation?

In a word, Dad, there simply is no remotely plausible explanation for all the evidence of the Resurrection except admitting that it in fact occurred the way the disciples said it occurred. I agree with you that this is, on one level, hard to believe because it goes against what we see every day: dead people stay dead. But I don't think we can use our general ordinary experience to rule out the possibility of something radically extraordinary happening, if, in fact, we have good evidence to suggest this.

Consider this: is there any ordinary thing which exists which wasn't extraordinary when it first began to exist? Whether one accepts evolution or creationism, the appearance of the first giraffe or elephant, and certainly the appearance of the first homo sapien, would have looked pretty extraordinary to anyone around to observe it. Now that animals and people are commonplace, we do not regard them with such awe.

The Resurrection is just like this. The resurrected life of Jesus is the first instance of something which is going to in time be universal. He is the first illustration of what humans are going to be, of what they are divinely intended to be. He is, in fact, the first true human being.

Jesus is, if you will, the first butterfly to come out of the cocoon. It seems implausible to us now only because we are yet entrapped inside our cocoons. But caterpillars are meant to fly! Or to switch the illustration, Jesus is the first zygote to go full term and become a newborn baby. But if you never saw a fully formed baby, you'd have trouble believing that this microscopic, fertilized zygote could ever become one. We believe it now only because this extraordinary event is now ordinary to us. But is the resurrection of Jesus really any more miraculous than the miracle of the birthing process? It certainly seems more extraordinary now. But if I'm right, Dad, before long it will be the universal rule. We are all destined to be resurrected on the last day.

What is tragic though, and I need to close by telling you this, Dad, is that Scripture makes it clear that many of these zygotes will be aborted. All will be resurrected someday, but not all will be resurrected to the eternal life with God that God has always intended for us. To be "born again," now and in eternity, one must trust in the means of birth provided by God. To continue the illustration, the only umbilical cord we have with God is Jesus Christ. When we cut ourselves off from this lifeline, we are stillborn. (The word for hell in Greek is gehenna, which was a huge burning dump outside of Jerusalem. The image fits the illustration, Dad. Those who cause themselves to be aborted from God's

*plan make themselves into what humans were never meant to be —
refuse. They are stillborns, who have no place among the living.)*

*I encourage you, Dad — I implore you — don't cut yourself off from Jesus
Christ. Don't reject Him. All that you were meant to be, all the
longings of your heart, your need for love, for hope, for significance, for
happiness, all are fulfilled in a relationship with God through Christ.
You were made for this. God wants it for you. He suffered death on the
cross that you might have it.*

All that I say, I say out of my love and hope for you.

Love,

Greg

How can you believe that a man was God?

July 16, 1990

Dear Greg:

How is training for the 100k championships going? How are Shelley and the kids doing these days? Bring me up to date on everyone in your next letter.

I appreciate the love and care you expressed in your last letter. I'm sorry I don't share your optimism about the prospects for my conversion, but who knows? I must admit, however, that your arguments on the resurrection of Christ were surprisingly strong. This obviously is no "blind leap of faith" you've been making. If nothing else, our discussions are beginning to answer the question I've had for so long about how you could go through all the schooling you've gone through, at some of the best graduate schools in the country, and continue believing this Christianity stuff. Even if I can't agree with you, I must admit you stand on some pretty solid ground. It gives me a headache thinking about it because I think the event itself is so improbable. But there the evidence is!

I don't feel like trying to nitpick at your evidence for the Resurrection. I want to respond with a different approach. Suppose, for the sake of argument, that I conceded that Jesus did resuscitate or something. The grave was empty. That would be a strange event, for sure, but I'm wondering whether it alone proves that this man is everything the Christians want to make Him. I mean, I've heard of other people coming back to life. Does this prove that they're God?

Look, unexplainable things happen a lot in this world. Look at all those strange "UFO" markings over in England. Maybe what happened in the first century was that an unexplainable event occurred, and in the face of this the disciples kind of flipped out and thought that Jesus must be God. In fact, maybe it was only Paul who flipped out to this extent (he always struck me as a bit off his rocker anyway). I've heard that he was the one who first believed that Jesus was divine. The Gospels rather portray Jesus in more earthly terms, as a great man who could work wonders (something I'm willing to grant).

What I'm trying to do, Greg, is reconcile the force of your evidence with a worldview that makes more sense to me. Concluding that Jesus was God just doesn't. How can you believe that a man, a literal human being, was God? All the arguments in the world for the Resurrection stop short of making this acceptable. That just seems to be something out of pagan superstition. It's an utter contradiction! I know Christians hold to a trinity, that part of God was down here while part of God was up there, or something like that. But simply holding that Jesus was a faith healer, who somehow resuscitated, and whose followers (one in particular) then went overboard making claims about Him explains everything without requiring a belief in such impossible notions.

Let me know what you think of this.

Love always,

Dad

July 28, 1990

Hello Dear Father:

The family is all doing very well up here in "cool" Minnesota. My training for the 100k is going OK, but I'm lucky if I get in 40 miles a week which is about half of what is generally regarded as a minimal amount of training for this event. The kids are jumping in races here and there when they feel like it. The other week we went to a track meet. Nathan was too young to participate in any events, but wanted a ribbon very badly. So I convinced one of the officials to give him one if he could run (and/or walk) halfway around the 400 meter track. Well, he took off like it was the Olympics. But, not knowing where the half-way point was, he ran the whole thing. About half way around some people in the stands noticed this little four-year-old accomplishing this exhausting feat and started cheering him on. By the time he was coming down the homestretch the whole crowd was on its feet cheering, and the officials put out a tape for him to break when he crossed the finish line. It was his moment of glory! I've never seen him look prouder. The official awarded him a first place ribbon.

Well, I'm happy to see you're willing to at least tentatively grant that Jesus rose from the dead. But you don't think this proves His divinity. You suspect that this belief was a piece of superstition that originated with Paul. This may surprise you, Dad, but I don't agree with you. Surprised? There are, I think, several considerations which count against your view, considerations that at the same time further substantiate the conclusion that Jesus Christ is God incarnate.

First, I think it is a mistake to hold that Jesus is seen as divine only in Paul's letters. It's true that Jesus Himself never comes out and explicitly says He is God in the Gospels, but He is everywhere portrayed in terms that come to the same thing. He says things like "If you see Me, you see the Father," "Honor Me even as you honor the Father," and "I and the Father are one." A good Rabbi (who was only a good human Rabbi) in the first century would never have spoken like this.

Moreover, Jesus makes Himself the object of faith, consistently saying such things as "believe in Me." He everywhere equates believing in Him with believing in God, rejecting Him with rejecting God. "He who believes in Me believes in the Father who sent Me." Even in His great "Sermon on the Mount" where the liberals say we find the "great human teacher," we find Jesus saying things like "Blessed are you when you are persecuted for My sake." Who does He think He is? A Rabbi is supposed to say, "Blessed are you when you are persecuted for God's sake."

On top of this, Dad, we find the disciples calling Jesus "Lord" (Kurios) which is the Greek equivalent to Yahweh, the name of God in the Old Testament. The doubting Thomas, on seeing Jesus, cries out, "My Lord and my God" — and Jesus doesn't correct him. And we find the disciples and others worshiping Jesus in the Gospels, something Jews would never do to anyone other than God! No, the Gospels present a "fully divine" Jesus.

Dad, do you remember when we used to attend that Unitarian church together? Do you remember when that professor preached a sermon entitled "Why Socrates Was a Greater Man Than Jesus"? We were both a bit taken back by it. He argued that Socrates was a greater man than Jesus because, while Socrates brought out the best in other people, Jesus "actually gave the impression that He was divine, even God." I think this professor was right in his assessment of the situation (though wrong in his conclusion). The Gospels force these two options: either Jesus was in fact divine, or He was not a very good person. We lock people up who say the things Jesus said!

Now, what makes all of this most remarkable, Dad, is that we are dealing with first-century Jews here. Jews were (and are) not like other ancient pagan cultures who believe in many gods, some who could come down to earth and take human form at will. No, at the center of the orthodox Jewish faith is the belief that there is only one God and that He is infinitely above human beings. If there is anything antithetical to their centuries-old faith it is the belief that God became a man!

Yet here we find just such a notion painted across the pages of the Gospels and the Epistles of the New Testament. A mere 15 years after Jesus lived we find Paul incidentally characterizing all Christians as those who worship Christ (1 Cor. 1:2). He quotes a hymn that had already been established in the church tradition which says that Jesus was equal with God (Phil. 2). And at a number of points he calls Jesus "Lord" (Yahweh) and "God" (e.g., Rom. 9; Titus 2).

All of this raises a perplexing historical question: whatever could have convinced these Jews that Jesus was in fact God incarnate? What on earth could have led these Jews to do what their entire culture prohibited them from doing — worshiping a man? What must Jesus have been like, what character must He have had, what claims must He have made, and what incredible deeds must He have done, to convince these orthodox Jews that He was everything their faith said a man could never be?

According to the Gospels, it wasn't the "resuscitation" of a corpse which convinced them that Jesus was God incarnate; it was the Resurrection of a man who had already embodied the kingdom of God—its love, teachings, and power—during His life. It was the Resurrection of a man who had already made astounding claims for Himself. And it was the Resurrection of a man who never did henceforth die. If Jesus had later died, the whole thing would have fallen to pieces. But He didn't. He ascended to heaven. (If this isn't true, one must answer the questions of where Jesus was "hiding" during the entire period of the early church; why and how the disciples would lie, and then die for their fabrication; and why this lie was never exposed, or even suspected, by anyone.)

My point, Dad, is that the Resurrection and deity of Christ are two sides of the same coin. It is as impossible to explain why the disciples believed one as it is to explain why they believed the other—unless we accept the Gospel accounts on face value. In fact, I'd go so far as to say that even if we didn't have the Gospels to inform us, we'd have to speculate that Jesus must have made the sort of claims and done the sort of deeds which the Gospels attribute to Him just to explain how the early Christians came to be convinced that He was everything we find Him being in the Epistles!

Now, is the belief that Jesus embodies God's presence in human form a contradiction, as you suggest? On what basis can anyone maintain this? It would be a contradiction only if being God by definition ruled out being human, and vice versa. But do we know enough, through our own little reason, about the nature of God, or the nature of humans, to conclude this? I think not. The only way we could know the nature of God is by God Himself telling us, and all the evidence suggests that Jesus Christ is just the place where this "telling" is done.

The Incarnation is, I grant, paradoxical, for we cannot understand how it is true. But it is not contradictory, for it is not nonsense to hold that it is true. The analogy that is frequently used by theologians is that physicists say something similar about the nature of light. It can be proven that light has both wave and particle-like features. But this is paradoxical, for we have no way of conceiving how something could have both of these features simultaneously. But since the evidence for both features is incontrovertible, physicists yet assert that it is, in fact, true.

Something similar may be said of the Trinity, which you also raised in your previous letter. This is not a belief that "part of" God was a man while "part of" God was in heaven. God is Spirit, and thus can't be "divided up." Rather, this belief is (among other things) the belief that God fully exists as transcendent Father, while God fully exists as Incarnate Son, while God also fully exists as indwelling Spirit (in the hearts of believers). God exists, and eternally has always existed, in three different ways. That's what the doctrine of the Trinity comes to.

Is this a contradiction? No, but it is paradoxical. We can't conceive how it is true, but there are good grounds for believing that it is true. And who would claim to know enough about God's nature by reason alone to say that God couldn't exist in this fashion? (In fact, in my book Trinity and Process *I argue that, on a strictly rational basis, one must maintain that any coherent understanding of God as self-sufficient and loving must embody some sort of "internal relationality"—which is exactly what the doctrine of the Trinity teaches. But that is a different matter.)*

I hope I've addressed your theory and your questions adequately. The bottom line is this: the evidence for the Resurrection and the deity of Christ stands or falls together, and there is simply no legitimate rational basis to the notion that the conclusion this evidence points to is inherently impossible.

I can tell you are taking the evidence seriously. I sincerely hope you follow it through to its only viable conclusion. Make Jesus the Lord and Savior of your life.

With love and hope,

Greg

PART III

QUESTIONS
ABOUT
THE BIBLE

Why does God make believing in Him so difficult?

August 21, 1990

Dear Greg:

Recent events bring up my old problem with the way God runs His show. Here's this madman Saddam Hussein bulldozing over the Kuwaiti people, raping their women and killing children in the process, and God sits on His hands. I know you answer this objection with your theology of freedom and spiritual warfare, but I bet if you polled all the people on the planet, including most of the people in Iraq, 99 percent would be in favor of temporarily bypassing whatever rules God has established about freedom in order to put this bastard six feet under! It would be a smaller sacrifice than the sacrifice God is going to make if He doesn't do this! Why do we little humans see what God doesn't? Why doesn't God run things more democratically!

Well, that's not really the problem for today. We've already hashed that over pretty well. I've got to address your stuff on the Resurrection and divinity of Jesus. I again have to admit that your arguments are very persuasive. At the least, I have no good arguments against them. But to be honest, in some ways the force of your arguments aggravate me. Nothing seems to fit. I mean, I can't begin to refute your arguments, but they still leave me in a position where I'd have to stretch myself beyond what I'm capable of to believe them. Why is this?

Why does God put us in a position where we have to *try* to believe in Him? Why does He toy with mankind, teasing us with evidence that's good enough to make us uncomfortable, but never coming directly out and making Himself clear? What's so great about "faith" that He desires it above an *obvious* revelation of Himself? And when He does reveal Himself—supposedly in the

Bible—He does so many damn bizarre things that no one who wasn't there to see it can be expected to believe it. Yet "salvation" supposedly hangs on this! Why do people have to believe things and accept stories that they'd never accept under ordinary circumstances in order to be saved? This isn't exactly fair.

So if I want to avoid hell, I presumably have to believe that a snake talked to Eve, that a virgin got pregnant from God, that a whale swallowed a prophet, that the Red Sea was parted, and all sorts of other crazy things. Well, if God wants me so bad, Greg, why does He make believing in Him so damn impossible? He gives an evidence here, an evidence there—enough to get us wondering—but then He throws in these other bizarre things which we can't possibly be expected to take seriously! If there were only the evidence, or only the crazy stuff, I'd have no problem. But combined, it's most aggravating!

It seems to me that an all-powerful God could do a much better job of convincing people of His existence than any evangelist ever does, and even better than all your arguments do. Hell, just write it across the sky, nice and big: "Here's your proof, Ed. Believe in Me or go to hell! Sincerely, the Almighty." You wouldn't have to spend an afternoon arguing history to me. I'd be on my knees!

I suppose it's for the better, but the more convincing you sound, the more ticked off I seem to get. And I've found myself recently thinking about all this material too much, which means I walk around here in a state of frustration. I don't have a clue as to what you could do about this. Maybe tell your "Spirit" who is supposedly quietly chipping away in my heart to come out of the dark and write in the clouds! Short of that, I think I'm destined to be an intrigued but frustrated skeptic, and your optimism about me is doomed to disappointment.

Sincerely yours,

Dad

September 6, 1990

Dear Dad:

I think I share much of your antipathy toward Saddam Hussein, but not the theological conclusions you draw from him. Get mad at Hussein. Blame him, and blame the power of evil which is behind him (but also behind the U.S. and other countries which are not blameless in these circumstances). But leave God out of the picture — except to call for help! He's more angry and sorrowful about the situation than any human could ever be. After all, our very sense of moral indignation comes only from Him. So He's on the side of righteousness, justice, and peace.

All I can say, Dad, is that if I can ever get you to channel that fire of yours in the right direction, you're going to make one heck of a prayer warrior! I'd love to see you get as angry at Satan as you get at God.

Well, to turn to the substance of your letter, I want first to thank you for your honesty. And thanks for taking my arguments so seriously. I really appreciate the respect I have always sensed from your writings. I've never felt like you just dismissed offhand what I had to say.

I'm sorry you're feeling frustration over all this, but then again I'm not. From my perspective, it's a positive thing. Changing something as fundamental as one's worldview is never easy — especially when you've held it for as long as you have. The mind, and even the heart, is torn in two directions at once. This is what psychologists call "cognitive dissonance." On matters of supreme importance, it's positively painful.

Not that it will be much consolation, but I think I know a bit how you feel. I told you some time ago about my experience walking back from an astronomy lab at the University of Minnesota. In my mind all the evidence for and against the existence of a loving Creator waged war. With varying degrees of intensity, that war raged in my head for a good six months. I've never been so thoroughly miserable.

But that was not the last time I felt like that. Throughout my graduate schooling there were several occasions when my faith was on the line.

121

I'd confront new evidence or new perspectives which seemed to contradict what I believed. And, for a while, my evangelical faith would go into a sort of "state of suspension." That's "cognitive dissonance." You're caught between two worldviews. In fact, to be perfectly honest with you, I still experience this "suspension" whenever I read about tragedies happening to children. The suffering of kids just rips me apart! When a young boy named Jacob Wetterling was abducted up here last year, I went through a long period of time when I would, on and off, get mad at God and question His integrity. Intellectually, I can fit such events into a coherent theistic worldview. (It was precisely by wrestling in my "suspension" with such events that I arrived at my present worldview—the spiritual warfare business, etc.) But emotionally, one can't see the nightmare of the whole thing and not temporarily rage. In a fallen world like this, worldviews are going to collide for thinking people.

So don't let my apparent certainty in our dialogue fool you. I'm a convinced Christian for sure: in the light of the evidence, and under the impact of the Spirit's working in my heart, I could not be otherwise. But faith has never come easily for me either. I saw and heard myself all over the pages of your last letter. Christianity isn't a giant "answer machine" (though fundamentalists try to make it that). To live is to live amidst questions and contradictory conclusions.

Well, the question you raised in the last letter was sort of a "meta-question": why do we even question? Why is faith so difficult? Why isn't God more obvious? I want therefore to provide a framework in which the questions you have make sense—that is, make sense of the fact that you have questions. If the Christian view of things can make sense of why the dilemma is here, it has, I think, gone one step further in resolving the dilemma.

Think for a moment, Dad, what would happen if God did what you asked Him to do in your last letter—if God individually wrote a message in the clouds for every person alive. What if He wrote "Jesus is My Son. Believe in Him or perish"? Would all people now put their love and trust in Jesus Christ? I suspect not. When Jesus was here on earth and did all His miracles, those who didn't want to follow Him still doubted. When the Father spoke from heaven "this is My beloved Son," those who didn't have a heart to believe said, "It thundered." And even when Jesus rose from the dead, there were a number of Roman guards who witnessed it, and yet they joined in with the religious leaders' conspiracy to cover it up!

It was just the same way in the Old Testament. Here God tried "the direct approach," but it failed miserably. He sent the plagues on Egypt to free the Israelites, but they soon doubted Him again. He sent them food straight from heaven, but many still rebelled. He continuously led them by a cloud during the day and fire at night, but many still questioned Him. He personally gave them, in great detail, all the directions they needed to be related to Him (the Law of the Old Testament — there's over 600 of them), but they broke every one. And even when they did keep all the "rules," the Law of the Old Testament failed to achieve what God wanted to achieve with the Israelites — a loving, trusting relationship.

There are many reasons for this, I suspect, but four come immediately to mind. First, the impression stupendous events have on us is rarely permanent. The impression fades with time. I have myself seen God do some incredible things with people, but in the weeks, months, and years after the event, the force of the initial impression wears off. Precisely because the event is extraordinary, the mind seems to remember it more like a dream than a real event. It doesn't continue to impact life. If a person does base his faith on miracles, he needs a steady diet. But then the miracles stop being miraculous. (They end up being faked, which is what happens with most of these faith-healing evangelists on TV.)

So even if God did address everyone with a message in the sky, this might convert many at that moment, but the lasting effect would, I suspect, be nil.

Second, there's almost nothing which can't be explained in more than one way. The cloud which says "Believe in My Son" could be a strange cloud formation, a hoax, a demon, a hallucination. The voice which says the same thing could be thunder. Jesus' miracles could be tricks, coincidences, or, as the religious leaders of His day thought, demonic activity. Things can always be explained away. How did the earth get here? Maybe a big bang! How are humans capable of consciousness, freedom, love, etc.? Just complex chemicals in motion. The explanations don't have to be good, just possible . . . and sometimes not even that! How did the disciples come to believe that Jesus embodied God's presence? Any guess will do for some.

Third, divine things are not as clear in this world as they might otherwise be because our world is, as I've argued before, caught in the crossfire of a spiritual cosmic war. There is an enemy of human souls which utilizes his destructive power to blind the eyes and ears of people (2 Cor. 4:4). So there's evidence of good, but also evidence of evil, which clouds every issue. And some of the time when things are not "clear" to people, it's not because the issue itself isn't clear; it's because their mind, deceived by the will of demonic forces or their own evil-bent free will, is cloudy. God can holler all He wants, but if people are covering up their ears, they cry out "why doesn't God talk?"

Finally, even when God's "direct approach" seems to work, it doesn't. God desires a loving, trusting relationship with us. We were created to this end. But does parting a Red Sea do that? Does speaking from the clouds do that? Does opening up the earth and swallowing the ungodly do that? He tried all of these and they didn't work. At best they can wow or scare people into submission (and that only temporarily). They can coerce obedience. They can temporarily modify behavior—including the fear-filled words "I love you." But they do not produce love. *If God were to answer obviously all our prayers, if He were a genie in a bottle granting our every wish, this would only mean that we'd use Him, not love Him. He'd be, as I said once before, a "cosmic vending machine." And He'd have a world full of spoiled, unloving children on His lever.*

Love must be chosen. It must be free, and it must be from the heart, without external motivations. But, quite frankly, it's very difficult for an all-powerful God to behave in such a way that love can occur with these qualities. If He uses the "direct approach"—to the point where an alternative explanation is not possible (if it's possible to do this), and continuously enough so it doesn't fade from our memories—He only succeeds in blowing us over or in spoiling us with a magical genie.

124

So God settles on a "middle of the road" program. He is present enough so that those who want to experience Him can experience Him, but absent enough so that those who don't want to experience Him aren't forced to — and they're actually in a sense justified in their complaint over God's absence! God is obvious enough so that those who want to see Him can see Him, but hidden enough so that those who don't want to see Him can avoid Him — and be in a sense justified in their complaint about His secrecy. Love requires both evidence and hiddenness.

Blaise Pascal put it this way: "God gives enough light to enlighten the elect, enough darkness to blind the reprobate." His whole book Pensees *is on this issue and is worth looking at. It's brilliant.*

The long and short of it, Dad, is that faith is more than a historical hypothesis. It is also a decision: a moral decision. The question is not only, "Do you rationally see why you should believe?" but also "Do you want to believe?" There's plenty of solid evidence for anyone who wants to believe, but enough faith is required to still render it a moral choice and not a coerced decision. God desires faith because He seeks love from responsible people, not forced behavior from robots.

Now I didn't specifically address your question about all the bizarre stories in the Bible, but I think I'd like to pass on that for now because it's not really central here. As important as those issues are, salvation isn't about believing in a talking serpent who deceived a woman, a giant fish who swallowed a man, or a sea that parted. It's about recognizing your need for the Savior, the Lord Jesus Christ. Much of the material in the Bible only begins to make sense after one's heart has been touched by the Lord.

If you can, then, "suspend" your judgment on those issues and consider strongly the issue of the Lordship of Christ, His deity, His life, and His resurrection. The evidence is irrefutable — but not coercive. A decision still has to be made. I pray that you make it.

With love,

Greg

Why do you think the Bible is inspired?

September 27, 1990

Dear Greg:

I'm afraid I just can't "suspend" my judgment on all the stories in the Bible. For me, Christianity stands or falls as a whole. It's a package deal. You can't ask me only to consider your strong arguments and bypass your embarrassing material. For me, to believe that Jesus is the Savior of the world goes hand in hand with believing in a book that has got some very strange stories in it. Problems with the book are therefore problems with the Savior.

So I again ask you to answer me this: how can anyone be expected to believe that a serpent talked, that a man was swallowed by a whale, that an ax-head floated, that a giant sea parted, that a man grew stronger the longer his hair became, and other such nonsense? How can anyone be expected to believe that all of this is literally "the Word of God"? If you read it in any other book, you wouldn't give it a second thought! I remember all these things primarily from my days as a Catholic, and I was disturbed by them then, even when I was "trying" to believe.

So, while your material on who Jesus was is admittedly compelling, I regard all of the other nonsense in the Bible as being a mark against it. Enough for now.

Love always,

Dad

October 13, 1990

Greetings, my skeptical Father:

My big race is only three weeks away, and I'm psyched! I'm going to hop into the Twin Cities marathon tomorrow with a friend for about 22 miles as a tune-up. Then I'll take it easy until the race. I'll let you know how it goes.

OK, you insist on addressing all the puzzles of the Bible. My reason for asking you to "suspend" judgment on this material was not because it's embarrassing to me but only because it's not central to Christianity; it's not part of the relationship with God which makes a person whole. This is the heartbeat of the Christian faith. The case for who Jesus was, I want to insist, stands or falls on its own. The inspiration of the Bible is a different, secondary matter. The reason I insist on this is because my strongest reason for believing the Bible to be "the Word of God" in the first place is a result of my already believing that Jesus Christ is Lord. Let me explain.

Several times in my rather "liberal" education I was, like you, inclined to just see the Bible as a human book. Some of the stories, I grant, are the sort of stories you would ordinarily see as fabrications if you read them in any other book. I also confronted problems with the texts which I couldn't explain, apparent contradictions, archeological discrepancies, etc. But I kept coming back to a belief that the Bible is God's Word, not because I could eventually explain all the problems, but because only this belief is consistent with a belief that Jesus is the Lord Almighty in human form.

My thinking goes along these lines, Dad. On the basis of reasons given in previous letters, I am convinced that the Gospels give us a fairly reliable historical portrait of Jesus and that Jesus Christ is the Incarnate Lord. This implies, it seems, that He doesn't make mistakes, at least not when He's teaching central things about God.

But if there's anything clear about Jesus' teachings in the Gospels it's that He clearly believed that the Old Testament was God's Word. This conviction runs throughout all of His teachings, and He bases His own self-understanding on it. What is more, Jesus clearly commissioned His disciples to teach with the same authority He Himself taught. He promised them that the Holy Spirit would come upon them and help them recall what He said and did, help them interpret who He was, and help them speak and write in such a way that others would believe on Him through them (John 14–16). Again, I'm not trying to quote the Bible to prove the Bible. I'm still just treating the Gospels as "basically reliable" documents.

So, though I at times had a lot of trouble making sense of the Bible, I always came back to this dilemma: how can I call Jesus "Lord," and yet correct Him on a central part of His theology? I may not understand much of the material in the Bible, but I am convinced that I cannot exalt my own reasoning above the authority of Jesus for this reason.

This, in a nutshell, is why I'd like you to consider the Lordship of Christ on the evidence I've given you, apart from my ability (or lack of it) to make sense of the troubling parts of the Bible. The way knowledge progresses in every field is working from the known to the unknown, the clear to the unclear. I'm asking you to start with what is clear (the Lordship of Christ) and then working to understand the unclear (the Bible).

The evidence for the Lordship of Christ, then, is my most compelling reason for accepting the Bible as God's Word. But it isn't my only reason. Let me give you several others.

First, the Bible contains a good deal of fulfilled prophetic material which is explainable only on the supposition that this book is God's Word. For example, running throughout the Old Testament narrative are prophecies about the coming Christ, prophecies which are fulfilled in the New Testament. Thus, to give but a few examples, the Old Testament foretells His place of birth as Bethlehem (Num. 24:17, 19; Micah 5:2 and others); His lineage from Abraham, Isaac, Jacob, and David (Gen.12:3; 21:12; 2 Sam. 7:13); His forerunner, John the Baptist (Isa. 40:3; Mal. 3:1); His vicarious suffering and death (Isa. 53); His crucifixion, before crucifixion was a mode of execution (Ps. 22:16; Zech. 12:10); His execution with common criminals (Isa. 53:9, 12); and His divinity (Isa. 9:6; Jer. 23:6; Micah 5:2; etc.). How is this to be explained? It goes miles beyond what "chance" would warrant.

What is more, there are many other fulfilled prophecies on other matters in Scripture. Let me give you one noteworthy example. The city of Tyre was a thriving seaport in the time of Ezekiel (around 580 B.C.). By inspiration, Ezekiel prophesies a number of things about this seaport that one couldn't have possibly just surmised at the time by looking at it. He prophesies that Nebuchadnezzar II, a Babylonian king, would overthrow the city (Ezek. 26:8), which was, after a 13-year siege, eventually fulfilled.

Ezekiel further prophesies that many nations would wage war with Tyre (26:3), something which was fulfilled throughout the next several centuries. He then states, most remarkably, that the city would finally be totally destroyed, made "flat as a rock," that fishermen would spread their nets over where she used to reign, and that she would never again be rebuilt (Ezek. 26:4-21). Who could have guessed this? Yet, all of this was, in subsequent centuries, precisely fulfilled.

In fact, Ezekiel even says that the debris from this city would be pushed into the sea (26:12). What an odd prediction to make about any city, let alone a thriving metropolis like Tyre. But several hundred years after this prophecy, it was fulfilled in detail. Alexander the Great laid siege to the city. The inhabitants fled to an island, just off the coast (which was part of their territory). Alexander couldn't invade it with a naval fleet, so he pushed the debris of the city into the sea to form a causeway to it! That's part of the reason it got so flat! Today where the ancient city used to be there are simply some small fishing villages where fisherman, as predicted, hang out their nets to dry on the flat rocks. The city itself is somewhere in the Mediterranean Sea!

I think that's a pretty impressive prophecy, Dad. And there are numerous others similar to it in the Bible. Does this not suggest that more than human authorship is at work here?

There are other reasons for holding the Bible, in spite of its "troublesome parts," to be inspired. It has, as I mentioned some time ago, time and again proven itself to be archeologically accurate. Even Time *magazine (Dec. 1974), in an article about Bible archeology, stated that "the Bible is often surprisingly accurate in historical particulars, more so than earlier generations of scholars ever suspected." And the article* concludes by saying, "After more than two centuries of facing the heaviest scientific guns that could be brought to bear, the Bible has survived—and is perhaps the better for the siege." There is no other ancient work about which this could be said.

There is also a unity to the Bible, Dad, that defies naturalistic explanations. From Genesis to Revelation we find the common unifying theme of God's loving pursuit of humanity, and humanity's resistance to Him. Amidst the incredible diversity of authors, perspectives, cultures, circumstances, times, worldviews, and literary genre, the Bible constitutes a unified song about redemption. In the same way that the diversity of Scripture testifies to its diverse human authorship, doesn't the overarching unity of Scripture testify to an encompassing, divine authorship?

And finally, there is the experience of the inspiration of Scripture, an experience testified to by Christians throughout the centuries. For one who has experienced the transforming power of the message of this "library," the "troublesome parts" of Scripture are minor. Jesus told a parable once of a man who found a jewel in a field and thus went out and bought the whole field to have it. Something similar is true of Scripture. The theme of redemption, and the Christ it presents, changed my life—and is still doing this. It seems natural for me to "buy the whole thing." I, with you, can't make heads or tails of some parts of it, but the transforming experience and solid evidence supporting its inspiration are simply too strong to be overturned by this occasional bewilderment.

Think about it, Dad. Better yet, start to read it, and talk to its Author while you're doing it. What have you got to lose?

Love always,

Greg

CORRESPONDENCE 20

Isn't the Bible full of myths and God's vengeance?

October 30, 1990

Dear Greg:

By the time you get this letter your race will be over. I hope it went well, as well as running 62 miles can go! If I could, I'd ship you my Jacuzzi to relax in afterward, but I'm afraid that's a bit out of the question. Why not just tack on a couple of extra miles and finish up at our house?

A few letters ago you talked about "cognitive dissonance," and that's exactly what I have. You give the best reasons imaginable for believing the most unimaginable things! A first-century Jew rose from the dead and was God. A book that tells me that a whale swallowed a man is God's Word. Who can believe it? But the way you argue, who can *not* believe it? It gives me a headache.

Help me in my dilemma. You give very good evidence for believing in the Bible, but the Bible is just too bizarre to believe. Do you take it all to be literally true? Do you take every word of it to be infallible? Square with me, Greg. Do you really believe in the talking snake stuff? Do you take all of this nonsense seriously?

And then there's this problem. You have talked so much about the love of God, etc. But the God I recall in the Old Testament is anything but this! Didn't He wipe out the entire planet with a flood? Quite a temper He's got! And didn't He order the extermination of the Canaanites — women and children included? And didn't He incinerate Sodom and Gomorrah? This doesn't seem like your all-loving God.

And, finally, there is this problem. I don't know much about this, but I've heard that none of the authors of the Old Testament books are the ones the books say they are. I've heard that a bunch of different people wrote the "five books of Moses," that Solomon couldn't possibly have written all his proverbs, etc. But then, later on, someone put the stuff all together and attributed it all to these figureheads. So if Jesus thought the Old Testament was the very Word of God, maybe He was wrong after all? So maybe He was either wrong in making divine claims for Himself, or the disciples were wrong in saying He did make these claims. And maybe He didn't rise from the dead? (But then what do I do with the evidence?) Or maybe we even went offtrack a long time ago in thinking that God was even personal? Ahhh!

Like I said when we began this whole correspondence, I don't know for sure what I do believe. I only have questions.

With sincere perplexity,

Dad

November 6, 1990

Dear Dad:

I'm in pain. A great deal of pain. I'm just beginning to be able to walk upright. I have four black toenails. One virtually exploded on me during the race. My shoe is more red than white now. And my knees, my poor, poor knees. I swear, I shall never do anything this foolish again (till next year?).

But I did OK, and, believe it or not, it was a great experience! Does that cause "cognitive dissonance"? I feel close to God toward the end of these races in a way I don't feel anyway else (probably because I'm so close to death!). I ended up as the 7th American and 23rd overall. Considering this was a World Championship, I'm very happy with it.

The conditions favored me a great deal as we had to run the whole race into a "rushing mighty wind" — gusts up to 35 miles an hour! This killed off a lot of the petite world-class runners, but favored my (much) heavier build. In better conditions, I'd have faired much worse.

Well, on to much more important matters. Dad, I do take the entire Bible seriously. How can I do otherwise if Jesus Christ is my Lord? He took it seriously, so must I. I'm thus prepared to accept stories as true which I otherwise wouldn't accept. But there are several considerations which alleviate the difficulty of this somewhat.

First, realize that humanity was in a very different situation back then than we are today. Hence, God's mode of operation was quite different back then than it is today. If we didn't have the fossil record, I'd have a hard time believing that the earth was once inhabited by creatures as tall as huge buildings — because I've never seen anything like this. All this dinosaur talk sounds like a King Kong piece of fiction. But because the evidence says so, I believe it. It's just the same with the Bible. We don't today normally see the sort of strange and miraculous activities the Bible speaks of, but if the evidence suggests that it was in fact like this, if we have reasons for accepting it, why not? The Resurrection of Christ, archeology, prophecies, etc. are, I contend, just those reasons.

Secondly, realize that the narratives of the Bible are selective. They are in the Bible precisely because they are unusual. God parted the Red Sea once. He operated in the very strange way He did with Samson once. He tailor-made a gargantuan fish (the Bible doesn't say "whale") to swallow a rebellious prophet once. Given the total scope of history, the spectacular deeds of Yahweh in the Old Testament are rare. But they're collected all together in one library called the Bible, which is why it collectively reads like these things happened all the time.

Third, as I hinted in a previous letter, I see no reason why God would have to limit Himself to the genre of literal history in revealing Himself to us. There is no reason why certain sections of Scripture could not contain some symbolic elements. If utilizing the literary genres of myth or allegory would better express the point God is trying to make, then what would prevent Him from using them? Nothing.

133

So, Dad, taking the Bible seriously does not necessarily mean taking it all literally. This is not a new insight of mine. Throughout church history certain Christian leaders have suggested that certain elements of Scripture may not be intended to be taken literally. Perhaps, some suggested, the talking serpent was a literary device used by the Author to represent Satan. Perhaps the forbidden fruit represents temptation.

Authors in biblical times were not as infatuated with "literal facts" as modern authors tend to be. They frequently wove together history and allegory or history and myth to make a point. Ezekiel 19 is one case in point. The author tells literal history, but he does it by using symbolism. The end result is a story which has a literal point and must, as history, be taken seriously, but which can't be understood literally at every point. The idea that the Bible must be 100 percent literal if it is 100 percent inspired is a very recent, and quite misguided notion.

But immediately a question arises to our literalistic modern minds: how is one to distinguish between what is literal and what is symbolic? It was the fear of just this question which sent the Fundamentalists at the beginning of this century into a misguided insistence that everything in the Bible must be literally true (though even they take selective features as being figurative, such as God having feathers or blowing fire out His nose, things the Bible also says). It is a difficult question, but one upon which little hangs. It's all God's Word and must, therefore, be taken seriously. The question itself must be decided on the basis of a thorough literary analysis of the text: What did the author intend to say? And even the experts disagree. But again, little hangs on this.

So, Dad, if you have problems with a talking snake, don't let this problem keep you from getting the point of the story. The point is not that snakes talk. The point is that Eve succumbed to a lie about who God was, and who she was, and thus thought she could improve her lot by something she did. She stopped being OK with herself simply as what God had created her to be. God's grace wasn't enough. That is the point of the narrative, and that is the essence of all sin to this day. The story is incredibly profound! Whether the snake is literal or symbolic couldn't affect the point of the story less!

Now concerning the vengeance of God in the Old Testament, I'll admit that I share with you a great deal of bewilderment over this. But it helps me to try to put things in perspective. First, as I said earlier, it's always best to work from the known to the unknown. Jesus Christ is the person in whom God is fully revealed. This, for me, must be my central definition of God. Whatever else God is like, He can't be different than the God I encounter here. "If you see Me," Jesus says, "you see the Father" (John 14). If something in Scripture appears to contradict this, I must confess ignorance and suspend judgment. I don't always know why God did what He did in the Old Testament. But since I know on other grounds that God is all-loving and all-wise, I must simply trust that He had wise and loving reasons for doing what He did.

Secondly, we again have to remember that when we read the Old Testament, we're dealing with an entirely different world than our own. We have trouble even imagining what the ancient mind was like. It was as different from our own as is the most primitive aborigine mind-set different from our own. It was an intensely violent, power-driven world where "might was right" (maybe not so different from our own after all?). Life was cheap.

The Canaanites, for example, used to ritually sacrifice newborn babies by burning them alive. There's evidence that they would perform some "religious" ritual of tying together the legs of a woman in labor, and leaving her there until she died! These cultures would sometimes impale their conquered adult subjects and celebrate their victories by smashing the heads of their subjects' infants against rocks!

So, perhaps one of the reasons God had to use violence in the Old Testament was because violence was the only way of accomplishing what He wanted to accomplish. In the heat of battle, only bombs talk.

Another consideration is this: perhaps the death of certain people was, in certain circumstances, the lesser of two evils. Do we not also believe that death is sometimes preferable to life? If, with this, one considers God's universal perspective, one must ask not only what is the lesser of two evils for the individuals involved, but what is the lesser of two evils for the entire world throughout history? God has an agenda for all of history, and given the fallen, barbaric state of the world, sometimes the death of large groups of people is preferable to letting such groups (viz., the Canaanites) adversely affect God's overall plan of redemption. (In fact, the few Canaanites who lived, because of Israel's failure to exterminate them, caused incredible difficulties later on!)

One final consideration on this. If one believes in an afterlife, as I do, then the death of the Canaanites is not really the end of their life at all. It may be just the beginning of an eternal life with God. What God does for historical purposes is not necessarily an indication of how God judges people eternally. And in this light, the death of certain Canaanite people, especially the children, could be seen as an act of mercy. Perhaps they were spared the hellish life (and probably afterlife) they would have had if they had grown to maturity. This may seem insensitive (I feel insensitive just saying it), but it is so only from a strictly "this world" perspective.

Something similar could, I suspect, be said about the Flood. Humanity became unimaginably sinful. "Every imagination of their heart was evil," the Bible says. Mankind was like the Canaanites, but on a global scale. Try to imagine that! This grieved God, Scripture says, to the point where He almost wished He'd never created humans. Instead of abandoning the project altogether, however, He found one salvageable person, Noah. He decided to recreate humanity using him as the new Adam, as it were. In a sense, one might say that when existence is worse than nonexistence, God simply withdraws His gift of existence. This is what God did in the Flood. It is the extremity God was willing to go to in order to keep His plan of eventually having a people who share and reflect His eternal love and joy.

Finally, let me briefly address your questions about the authorship of the Old Testament. I would again argue, Dad, that this has little or no bearing on the inspiration of the Bible. For my part, I think the evidence indicates that Moses was the primary author of the first five books of the Bible, but it also seems clear that he utilized sources which predate him (like the Gospel authors did), and also that material was added to this work at a later date.

But what hangs on this? What if Moses were only a figurehead to the whole work? Does this put Jesus in error for following the tradition and referring to "the five books of Moses"? I think not. The same is true of Proverbs, the Psalms, or whatever books you wish. No one believes that Solomon handwrote every single proverb in the collection entitled Proverbs. But he is the traditional figurehead for ancient Semitic wisdom literature, so the works are collectively ascribed to him. So with David and the Psalms. Some of the Psalms even explicitly give a different author than David. But the work as a whole is referred to as "the Psalms of David" because he is the traditional figurehead behind ancient Semitic psalm writing.

I hope this clears things up a bit, Dad. It seems to me that a good many of your problems with the Bible arise from misconceptions about what kind of book the Bible is supposed to be. This is a common misunderstanding, even among Christians (which is where a good deal of all this "inerrancy" controversy arises). But once one gains a perspective on the issues, the issues are, I believe, comparatively minor.

So I encourage you, Dad, as I did before, to be patient with the perplexing parts of this God-inspired book and open yourself up to its transforming power. It really is inspired! If you let it, it will lead you into a relationship with the Savior.

As always, with love and hope,

Greg

Didn't the Catholic Church put the Bible together?

December 11, 1990

Dear Greg:

Let me again tell you how proud I am of your World Championship performance. I hope nothing is permanently damaged and that you finally got this craziness out of your system! I'm sorry to hear you and the family won't be able to come down. We were really looking forward to it. We miss you all so much. But we understand. When we win the state lottery, Jeanne and I will fly you all down every year!

On to theology. Greg, I almost hate to admit this, but you are starting to make sense! I'm beginning to think that most of my hang-ups about Christianity are the result of getting it from two wrong sources: the Catholic Church and the bozo preachers on TV (which I occasionally watch just for laughs). Your stuff on the Bible cleared away a lot of the fog I had in my head about the book. I still don't care for the Old Testament picture of God much, but I'm more willing to suspend judgment on it because of the perspective you've given me.

But another question has come to the surface as I read, and re-read, your last letter. I was taught in my Catholic days that the Protestants were mistaken in going by the Bible alone because it was the church that put the Bible together. Wasn't it the Catholic Church that decided what books got into the Bible and which books didn't? Didn't they do this sometime around the fifth century? The priest was teaching us this to convince us that Protestants owe it to Catholics that they have a Bible in the first place.

I'm wondering how this could be if this is God's Word. I mean, why would it take so long to decide, and how could God leave such an important decision in the hands of self-serving rascals? I've heard somewhere that it was left up to some council of bishops to actually vote on what books were and were not inspired! That doesn't seem like a very dignified way to establish the Word of God. How do you know if they were right? Maybe some "bad" books got in? Maybe some inspired books were left out?

And don't Catholics and Protestants still fight over this? Why does the Catholic Bible have more books than the Protestant Bible? Yet both claim to be "God's Word"! It just doesn't make sense to me.

So, while your presentation of Christ and the Bible have been very compelling to me, I still have a lot of hurdles to jump before I can leap onto your ship of faith.

All my love,

Dad

December 28, 1990

Dear Dad:

I hope you and Jeanne had a very nice Christmas. I'm again sorry we couldn't be with you. Next year for sure! We're starting a monthly savings account beginning January, and nothing is going to stop us. Not only do we want to see you and Jeanne, but our kids are driving us nuts because they want to go to Disney World!

I can't tell you how happy I am to see that you are starting to see the plausibility of Christianity. I've told you all along, Dad, you're a targeted man. God is not going to let you go. Between me and the Holy Spirit, you haven't got a chance!

Now onto your questions. I'm afraid you've again been given some misinformation — or you misunderstood the information you were given — about the process of canonization. It's true that no formal list of canonized books was drawn up until the fifth century, and it's true that there were a couple of books certain influential people squabbled over up to this time (and even a while thereafter). But the vast majority of the New Testament canon was settled in the second century. We can discern this just from the way early church fathers cite the New Testament as authoritative. Over 90 percent of the New Testament can be reconstructed from quotes of the early fathers up through the third century.

The only reason anyone even started worrying about an "official" canon was because a heretic, named Marcion, came along in the second century and formed his own tailor-made heretical canon. This guy hated Jews, and he hated the Old Testament, so he started his own branch of Christianity, excluding the Old Testament altogether (he said an evil god wrote it) and using only fragments of the New Testament. He'd cut and paste together portions out of each book to fit his aberrant theology.

Well, his movement started catching on, and in the face of this the church had to provide believers with an official teaching on what was and was not the true New Testament. It wasn't that the New Testament had to be established so much as it was that this false teaching had to be confronted. So official pronouncements were made. The first known "official" list of canonized books we have is the Muratorian canon, which dates about A.D. 170. The list we have here is almost identical to the one you find in every Bible today.

You see, Dad, the inspired works of the New Testament were received as such by people of faith almost from the start. There wasn't a whole lot of controversy about this. These works were circulated among all the churches, and gradually a pretty well-defined body of literature was generally recognized as the New Testament. Thus, the unofficial formation of the canon came first, followed by controversies like those of Marcion, then followed by official formations of the canon. Aside from the formal establishment of a few books which some regarded as questionable, the official canons didn't add a thing to what was already there.

Now in answer to your question of how we can know for sure that all the right books were included, and all the wrong books were omitted, I'm afraid I don't have a conclusive answer for you. I can't rule out the theoretical possibility that a certain book shouldn't have been included that was included (Luther suspected this about the Book of James). Nor can I conclusively rule out the possibility of an inspired book being left out that could have been included.

But I wouldn't lose sleep over this. Three considerations put me to sleep at night.

First, I have to believe in God's providence at some point along the way. If God took the time and effort to become Incarnate to save us, I have to believe that He'd also oversee the general process by which the information of this event is passed on to us. Jesus promised His disciples that the Spirit would inspire them and that the world would believe on Him through their word. If He inspired the work, I have to believe He'd make sure it became canonized. If a book did get "lost," I just have to believe it wasn't that crucial.

Second, the process of bringing inspired books together into a single canon was no casual affair for the early church. These people were dying for their faith, and so they wanted to make sure that everything they believed came from the mouth of God. No one wants to die for a lie. So they applied pretty stringent criteria on these books. Who wrote it? When was it written? Is its content consistent with other works acknowledged by all to be inspired? Has it been received by churches from the start as inspired? And does it have the transforming power of God's Word? They were in a better position than ourselves to answer most of these questions, and they had more to lose by answering these questions wrongly. So I feel pretty secure abiding by their decisions. Besides, these works now carry the testimony of Christians throughout history who believe them to be inspiring and life transforming. So if I happen to find a particular book not to be such, it seems most presumptuous of me not to suspect that the fault is more my own than the book itself.

Finally, even if one were to reject the few letters that were disputed in the early church (viz., those writings which weren't actually acknowledged by the church as a whole until the fifth century), not a great deal is lost in the New Testament. The New Testament forms an incredible monument which stays very much intact, even if some noteworthy stones are removed. Second Peter, for example, was disputed primarily because its style is so different from 1 Peter. This is easily explained (he tells us he enlisted the help of Silas in writing the first letter, 1 Peter 5:12), but even if one dropped out 2 Peter, what of any consequence would be altered? So with 2 and 3 John, James, Hebrews, and Revelation. These are very good books, and I'm glad they're in the canon. But the point is, nothing central to salvation hangs on their existence.

So, the notion that Protestants owe their Bible to the Catholic Church of the fifth century is a mistake. In fact, if one defines the Catholic Church by the line of popes which head it, it's very hard to argue that there even was an official Catholic Church before the sixth century (and probably even later).

Now, the issue you raised over the differences between the Catholic and Protestant Bibles has nothing to do with the issue of the canonization of the New Testament. The difference rather came about with Luther's break from the church in the sixteenth century. Up to this time there had been a body of literature, known as apocryphal literature, which accompanied the officially canonized literature of the Bible. There was a difference of opinion among church leaders about this literature. Some regarded the literature as having the same status as the biblical literature; some did not (an ambivalence we inherited from Judaism). So it was usually included in the biblical canon as "edifying" literature, but was not officially regarded with the same authority as the rest of the Bible.

With Luther's break with the church, however, the ambiguous status of the apocrypha had to be made clear, for a number of reasons. Chief among these was the fact that Catholic leaders wanted to quote this literature in support of some of their doctrines which Luther denied (e.g., purgatory). So Luther absolutely denied the canonicity of the apocrypha, and this forced the Catholic Church to the other extreme of absolutely affirming this literature. Both positions were "new" in the history of the church.

For my part, Dad, I am on the side of Luther. Without going into all my reasons for my position, I'd just say (a) neither Jesus nor His disciples ever cited the apocrypha as authoritative; (b) the apocrypha contains material which appears to contradict New Testament teaching; (c) the early church fathers rarely cited the apocrypha as authoritative; and (d) the quality of literature, I would argue, is on the whole significantly below that of the canonized literature.

But, as with the canonized books which were questioned in the early church, I would never lose sleep over this issue. Nothing much hangs on it. I wouldn't even mind endorsing the pre-Reformation view of the apocrypha. If someone finds this literature to be inspiring, edifying, and life transforming, great. I do not. Let each decide for himself.

The rub of the whole matter, Dad, is that the minor issues which surround the Bible never affect the central content and all-important message of the Bible. I would encourage you to just start reading it. You might want to begin with the Gospels, especially the Book of John. Set aside the issues and just try to hear what the work is saying to you. Allow the Holy Spirit to use the text to drive home to your heart what needs to be heard.

The thrust of the entire Bible, Dad, is to bring you into a loving relationship with Jesus. The Bible comes alive to the extent that a person meets Jesus through it.

With all my love and hope,

Greg

CORRESPONDENCE 22

Why are there so many differing interpretations of the Bible?

January 16, 1991

Dear Greg:

Well, I hope your new year is off to a good start. Thanks so much for your last letter. It cleared up a major misconception I had about how the Bible came to be. I still have trouble squaring the authority this book is supposed to have with the apparently haphazard way it was "officially" brought together. Why didn't God just drop it out of heaven? But it at least helps to know that it wasn't the product of a church I don't particularly care for.

The question I've had lately rides piggyback to the question I raised in my last letter. Greg, if the Bible is God's Word, why is it so unclear? You may say that it's not unclear, but if that were so, why are there so many differing interpretations of it? I mean, there are over 1,200 differing Christian denominations in America alone! Each claims to have "the correct" view of the Bible. How can this be? Can't God speak clearly? And how is a person without a Ph.D. in theology supposed to know who the hell is right?

Give my love to the wife and kids. Hope to hear from you soon.

Lots of love,

Dad

January 24, 1991

Dear Dad:

Dad, if you become half the Christian you are the skeptic, you're going to be one heck of a theologian! I'm beginning to wonder if there is going to be one objection to Christianity you aren't going to raise.

The problem of disunity among Christians is a perpetual thorn in the flesh for every Christian. Toward the end of Jesus' ministry He prayed that all believers might be united so that the world would know that Jesus was really sent by God (John 17). Well, we are not very united, and this, in part, damages our witness to Christ as Savior.

This isn't as much a commentary on the ambiguity of the Bible as it is a commentary on the sinfulness of the church. Most of the differences between churches, Dad, are more the result of pride, arrogance, greed, and a hunger for power than they are legitimate differences in interpreting the Bible. Christians are sinners, Dad, pure and simple. The bad side of this is that it hinders the work of God. The good side of this is that it reassures you and me that we'd fit right in! If it were some kind of holiness club, I'd be long gone.

None of this should really surprise us, though. There is hardly any biblical account of God ever accomplishing His purpose through someone who didn't do his best to botch it up! The Bible itself says that "God chooses the foolish things to confound the wise, the weak things to confound the strong" (1 Cor. 1:27, my paraphrase). So Abraham, for example, is God's man for the hour. And what does he do? He twice gives his wife away to sleep with a stranger to save his own neck! What a "man of God"! And David, the Bible says, is a man "after God's own heart." So he has sex with another man's wife, gets her pregnant, and has the husband killed so he can quickly marry her and cover up the crime. What a "saint"! And Israel, "God's elect nation," is throughout biblical history consistently rebelling against Him, chasing after false gods, and just generally screwing things up. And then there's the Christian church you see today. Nothing has changed, has it?

But in some ways that makes an important point, Dad. Paul at one point writes, "So God has demonstrated that all are under sin, so that He might have mercy on all" (Rom. 11). In a mysterious way, God uses the vehicles of His communication to demonstrate to all a universal truth: people are sinners in need of grace. Nowhere is this sinfulness more obvious, and nowhere is this grace more demonstrated, than in "God's people." Abraham, David, Israel, the church — if God can save and use sinners such as these, there is hope for all. When the intent of creation is finally achieved, Dad, God will be eternally displayed as the God of undying mercy in the face of human rebellion and sin. And the more clearly the latter is shown, the more clearly the former is revealed. Thus, He now works through the sinful church.

Most of the divisions in Christianity, then, are due to its sinfulness. But I'd be dodging your question if I said that all differences among churches are due to this. There are two further reasons for differences among churches. Neither, however, impugns the clarity of the Bible.

First, not all churches regard the Bible itself in the same way. Liberal churches don't regard it as "God's Word" in any definitive way. They feel free to reject aspects of it if they don't agree with it. Fundamentalists, at the opposite extreme, are so afraid of anything "liberal" that they tend to read the Bible "ahistorically." They try to make the Bible into a twentieth-century legal document.

Then there are the Catholics who see the Bible as but one of several sources of authority — the pope and church tradition being the other two. The Orthodox Church has the same perspective, but it doesn't accept the Pope. And then there are the Evangelicals who, like the Fundamentalists, view the Bible as God's Word, but they nevertheless hold that it should be read in its historical context. It is not a twentieth-century legal document.

This difference in perspectives clearly would prevent these different churches from working together in perfect harmony. As you could have guessed from the way I've been handling your previous questions, I am an Evangelical. *Unlike the Liberal church, I strive to regard the Bible with the same attitude Jesus exemplified toward it. Because I call Him*

"Lord," there is nothing which I can simply reject. Unlike the Funda-
mentalists, however, I see the value and necessity of reading the Bible in
the light of history. As you have seen, I am not opposed to the discovery
of "sources" in the biblical tradition, or of holding that certain parts
were not meant to be taken literally if the evidence points in this
direction. And unlike the Catholic and Orthodox Churches, I see no
good grounds for accepting anything outside the Bible as having an
authority which parallels the Bible.

These differences, clearly, are not the result of any ambiguity in the
biblical text itself. It is, in my estimation, the result of historical and
cultural influences coloring peoples' understanding of the status of the
Bible itself.

Secondly, there are, within each of these groups, differences of opinion
on how certain texts are to be interpreted. Does the Bible teach that the
bread and wine of Communion is a symbol of Christ's body and blood,
or the actual thing? Does the Bible teach that infants or adults should
be baptized? What does baptism symbolize? Does the Bible teach that
the church should be run from the top down (a hierarchical govern-
ment), or from the bottom up (a congregational government)? Should
people speak in tongues in church or not? Beyond the different ways of
viewing the Bible itself, these are the sorts of differences in biblical
interpretation which distinguish churches from each other.

Now I could give you my reasons for holding the particular theology I
hold on each of these issues, but far more important than this is the
realization that these differences are all but totally irrelevant next to the
central message of the New Testament which rings forth loud and clear:
Jesus Christ died for you and is the Lord and Savior of all who
believe!

Dad, a person isn't saved because of the view they hold of Communion,
or of church government, or what have you. A person is saved because
of his relationship to Jesus Christ — whether he is in a Liberal, Funda-
mentalist, Catholic, or Evangelical church, whether he holds to infant
or adult baptism, to a hierarchical or congregational form of govern-
ment, etc. God's Word is perfectly clear at least on this one central

point. It's no fault of the Bible if it didn't pre-address every doctrinal issue that was going to be raised in the church. It is, therefore, no fault of the Bible if it doesn't clearly answer every question we'd like it to address. And it is no fault of the Bible if people, under the influences of historical and cultural factors, read it in different ways. What is most important to hear can be clearly heard if a person's heart is open to it.

So I come to the same point I seem to come to in every letter, Dad. Let the issues rest for now, and consider your relationship to Jesus Christ. The truth and life of this relationship stand quite apart from all these other issues. Once you've entered this relationship and been nurtured in it a while we can, as you so desire, begin to address these other issues. They are important, for sure. But they are not "saving." And right now, I just want you saved! It's always only a prayer away, Dad.

With all my love and prayers,

Greg

CORRESPONDENCE 23

What about the "holy books" of other religions?

March 4, 1991

Dear Greg:

It was good to talk to you the other week. Sorry to hear that you guys have all been passing around the flu. People in Florida never get sick. Did you know that? I'm sure there are plenty of schools down here that would be glad to have you, Greg. Why not wise up and move!

I was, as I told you, a bit surprised but also impressed, to hear you harping on the church's sinfulness in your last letter. It seems to me that Christians are usually trying to paint this holy picture of themselves, but it's something anyone with half a brain can see right through. Look at this Jimmy Swaggart business. I always took this to be one more evidence that the church's message couldn't be correct, but you've pretty much ridden me of that assumption. If the message God is trying to convey to the world through the church is that we are all sinners, He's doing a mighty fine job!

I wonder, however, if you didn't minimize the blame which the Bible must take for the different views Christians have of it. Are questions about baptism and the like the only things Christians don't agree on? Didn't that group you used to belong to when you first became a Christian hold that the Trinity was wrong? Don't the Jehovah's Witnesses who come around here every so often say that Jesus wasn't God? These seem like pretty major disagreements, yet they also claim to be "going straight from the book."

This leads me to an even more fundamental question. All religions have their own "Bibles," don't they? How do you know that yours is the only true one? They, no doubt, have their own reasons for holding to the one they believe in, just like you do yours.

So how can you say yours is the one and only true one? It strikes me as a fairly narrow-minded position.

Well, enough for now. Take care of yourself, son.

Lots of love,

Dad

March 15, 1991

Dear Dad:

So people in Florida never get sick, do they? Seems to me they get plenty sick of the heat! I'll take the occasional runny noses.

OK, on to your questions. You are correct in pointing out that there are certain small sectarian groups which distinguish themselves from traditional Christianity by interpreting the Bible in such a way that they deny some central tenets of the faith. But these are generally regarded as "cults," and their very uniqueness is an indictment on them. Anytime anyone "discovers" some new "truth" in the Bible that no one else in church history has ever seen — and these sects are founded on just this assumption — one should immediately become suspicious. This is especially true if this "discovery" concerns something central to the faith.

It's not impossible, of course, but the church has had some brilliant scholars and pretty spiritual saints throughout its history, so if someone is going to claim that all of these people missed something central to salvation, he needs to make a very strong case that this is so. (It should also take a tremendous amount of evidence to come to believe that God would let His church exist in fundamental error throughout the centuries, up to the time of the all-important sectarian "discovery.")

150

None of these sectarian groups have ever come close to making such a case. In fact, their handling of the Bible is usually pretty uninformed and even bizarre. It has to be to get around teachings which everyone else who has ever read the Bible has regarded as being very clear. What really fuels their effort is a need to feel "elitist" in their beliefs. Some people just need to believe that they have something no one else has. This sentiment certainly dominated the aberrant group I belonged to in the '70s.

But the Bible itself can't be blamed for any of this. We wouldn't blame Shakespeare if some uninformed person who needed to feel special came up with some bizarre interpretation of Macbeth, *would we?*

Now about the "holy books" of the other religions, I would just say three things.

First, only a few major religions have "holy books" that claim to be "God's Word." The literature of most religions, Hinduism and Buddhism for example, is regarded by the religion's adherents as being sacred and full of wisdom, but in no sense infallible. So my stance toward these works is to read them and judge for myself to what extent each work contains "sacred wisdom." Sometimes they do, sometimes they don't. Even an adherent to the religion could say this.

Secondly, concerning the other religions who in fact have "competing Bibles," the most reasonable posture, I would think, is to work from the known to the unknown. Thus, I know why I believe in Christ, why I believe in the Bible, and what the Bible has done for my life. I have to start with this. When I judge "the competition" in this light, I arrive at the conclusion that, since they contradict the Bible on certain fundamental points, they cannot also be the Word of God. Like other religious literature, they may contain a great deal of human wisdom. But I cannot regard them as having the sort of authority Jesus invested in the Bible.

But, you asked, do these groups not have their own reasons for believing in their sacred books? Well, bring them on! I have read Islamic books trying to prove the inspiration of the Koran, *and Mormon books trying to prove the inspiration of the* Book of Mormon, *and frankly, I'm not impressed. They simply don't have the irrefutable character which the Resurrection or the fulfilled biblical prophecy have. What is more, since* both of these works (and others like them) contradict the Bible on fundamental matters, all my reasons for believing in the Bible also constitute reasons for not believing in them. So not only do they not have good grounds in favor of them, they have solid evidence against them as well.

Thirdly, it shouldn't surprise you, Dad, to find that there are other works which claim to be God's Word. For one thing, it simply reveals how hungry people are to hear God's Word. When a starving person doesn't have any real food to eat, he fantasizes a dinner of his own creation. As C.S. Lewis once remarked, "Myth points to reality." Myth expresses the heart's conviction that such and such should be real. If there is a genuine "Word of God," we should expect to find mythological approximations of it in cultures where it is absent, or at least where it isn't recognized for being what it is.

I don't think this is being narrow-minded, as you suggested. Narrow-mindedness does not attach to what you believe, but how you believe it. If I refused to consider any perspective, any religious book, and any philosophy which disagreed with my own, that would be narrow-minded. But just because I hold to a belief that disagrees with other perspectives, other religious books, and other philosophies doesn't itself make me narrow. No matter what you believe, Dad, there will always be more who disagree with it than who agree with it. "Truth is one, but falsehood is manifold."

Dad, the Bible itself tells us to "test everything. Hold on to the good" (1 Thess. 5:21). Subject any and all claims of revelation to the same test, and you find, I contend, that the Bible stands alone as the definitive "Word of God." All other works may, and do, have wonderful literary and philosophical insights within them. But they do not communicate to humanity the one thing that is most needful: the person of Jesus Christ.

Thanks for keeping the letters coming. I appreciate the opportunity to interact with you. One of these days we're going to hit the bottom of your "bucket of questions"—and you'll find smiling up at you from the bottom of that bucket the loving face of the Savior. He's going to say, "I've been waiting for you, Ed." I can't wait!

With all my love and hope,

Greg

PART IV

QUESTIONS
ABOUT CHRISTIAN
LIFE AND DOCTRINE

CORRESPONDENCE 24

Do all non-Christians go to hell?

April 4, 1991

Dear Greg:

Your approach to examining the "holy books" of other religions makes sense to me, but that's probably because I am a Western person familiar with the Bible. So, Greg, I'm not yet satisfied with your response. The root of my problem, I think, is that regardless of how much more reasonable the Bible is (to us!) to believe as God's Word than any other book, people are still going to believe in other books so long as it's part of their upbringing and culture to do so.

Now, on your account, does this not mean that these people cannot be saved? Isn't this what all "born-again" people believe? And doesn't this mean that these unfortunate people — who constitute the vast majority of the world — are in fact going to be sent to hell by your all-loving God? But how can this be since they had nothing to do with *when* they were born, *where* they were born, *what* culture they were born into, and even *who* they were born as! Yet, *these* are the sorts of things heaven and hell hang on. *These* are the factors which determine what sort of life philosophy a person is going to hold. Whatever free will we may in fact have, its scope of operation is *within* the limits set by *these* factors. So one's life philosophy, or one's salvation by your account, is not, after all, something we "freely" choose.

I guess I'm back to my old gripe about God's fairness. If the chance evil in our world is difficult to accept, the chance evil in eternity is utterly impossible to accept. How can one go to hell by the accident of where he happened to be born? How can there be one right way to God when there are so few who have the chance of finding that one way? How can heathen children go to hell just because they weren't born into a Christian home?

To be perfectly honest, Greg, I've always found the Christian doctrine of hell, and the belief that all nonbelievers are going there, to be one of the most ludicrous aspects of the entire religion. Maybe you can straighten out some of this.

Love always,

Dad

April 27, 1991

Dear Dad:

You certainly aren't out to make this easy for me, are you, Dad? Why can't you just feel the Spirit tell you it's all true and then convert! I'm just kidding. In truth, I admire your inquisitiveness and am enjoying the challenge of our dialogue.

Now you're raising, once again, a very good and extremely difficult theological issue. And I should maybe tell you right at the start that it's an issue about which there is a lot of disagreement, even among Evangelicals. So if you're looking for absolute certainty in resolving the issue, you're probably going to be disappointed.

My approach, as I've said over and over again, is to work from the known to the unknown, the clear to the opaque. What happens to all who die without Christ is opaque, and so I shall attempt to work toward a solution by starting with what is clear. When I do this, Dad, I discover five principles which affect my opinion on this matter.

First, if I have very good grounds for believing the Bible to be God's Word — the person of Jesus, fulfilled prophecy, personal experience, etc.—then I must, at the start, be willing to confess that this revelation may have teachings which are going to transcend my own rationality. In fact, I should expect such a revelation to be paradoxical at points. If it squared with what I already believed on every point, I'd have good reason to suspect that it was of a strictly human origin rather than divine.

The bottom line, Dad, is that reality is infinitely more complex than we can ever even imagine. There are perhaps billions of variables which affect God's interaction with us about which we have no conception (recall the analogy of the hut on Normandy beach caught in the cross fire which I used some time ago). And since our perspective on reality is so incredibly myopic, we must expect that we might, at points, simply have to trust that God will do the wise and just thing—though we don't see how what He's doing is wise and just. So if people go to hell that we don't think should be there, it may be because our perspective is "a bit" more limited than God's!

Second, I am certain that God is most decisively revealed in Jesus Christ. Nothing is more central to the New Testament than this. "If you see Me, you see the Father" (John 14:9-10). Thus, as I did with the issue of God's vengeance in the Old Testament, if there is something which to my reason does not appear to square with the revelation of God in Christ, I must simply be willing to put this "on suspension" for the time being. God may indeed appear vengeful and full of wrath, and nowhere more than with this doctrine of hell. This is what Luther called "the left hand of God." It is a mysterious side of God Luther did not understand. But what Luther did nevertheless understand was that the believer can with full confidence say, "no other God have I but Thee; born in a manger, died on a tree." However God may appear at times, He cannot be other than He is in Jesus Christ. Of this I am certain, though I may have to "suspend" judgment on all the "appearances."

A third principle of which I am certain as I work toward an under-standing of the issue you raised is that there is no salvation outside Jesus Christ. This also is perfectly clear in the New Testament. No one goes to (or "knows," "loves," or "believes in") the Father except through the Son: this is a dominant theme in the New Testament.

"There is no other name under heaven given to men by which we must be saved" (Acts 4:12). Sinners are only made compatible with God through the sacrifice of Jesus Christ. They cannot do it on their own. If one is saved, then, it is through Jesus Christ.

But there is also a fourth truth about which I am certain in the Bible, and that is that there are some people who did not know Jesus Christ personally or consciously, but who were nevertheless saved. We know of saints in the Old Testament who shall be in heaven, and the Bible even implies this about several individuals who were not even Israelites (e.g., Noah, Job, Melchizedek). How can this be if everyone who goes to the Father goes through Christ? How can this be if, in fact, Noah, Job, and Melchizedek were sinners in need of salvation just like everyone else?

The only solution I can see, Dad, is that the sacrifice of Christ embraces more than those who consciously embrace it. If people in the Old Testament, Jews and Gentiles, could be made right with God, then it can only be because God applied to them the blood of a Savior they were, for various reasons outside of their control, prevented from knowing. To "go through" Christ, then, cannot be exactly the same thing as "believing in" Jesus Christ. There apparently are people who are covered by Christ's blood who do not even consciously know Him.

This, I suspect, is what we must also say about small children who die, about retarded people, and about others who are prevented from knowing Christ through no fault of their own. God judges people according to their hearts according to the light of truth which they did have to respond to, and according to the faith which was (or was not) implicit in their hearts (Matt. 25; Rom. 2). So, Dad, He is a fair and just God. People don't go to hell "by accident."

Finally, there is one issue which is clear: that is that people who have not heard and believed in the Gospel are in grave danger. While there may be enough in the Bible to give us a small degree of hope for the unevangelized, there is nothing to give us any assurance about them. Indeed, everything we are told impresses on us an urgency about evangelizing them. All people need to hear!

So do all non-Christians go to hell? I can say with certainty that all without Christ are damned, but not that all without explicit faith in Christ are damned. I can say with certainty that all outside the faith are in danger and that only those who have an explicit faith are assured of salvation. But neither do I have a certainty that they are lost. I know of some cases (Old Testament believers, children, retarded people) where this is not true, and so I must in every instance simply leave it up to God to do what is just and right.

Resolve to know God only through Jesus Christ, Dad, and relax! If God is as He is revealed in His Son, He's going to judge the world in the best possible way. We'll see that someday. Your only concern should be that you are not among those who reject Christ of their own free will. Choose to believe! Receive Him as your Lord and Savior! Let hell be God's problem, not your problem.

With all my love,

Greg

How could an all-loving God torture people in an eternal hell?

May 12, 1991

Dear Greg:

I'm afraid I just have a little more difficulty "suspending" things than you do. Because I'm not yet 100 percent convinced that Jesus is God on earth, like you are, I can't so quickly find solace for the nagging questions I have about hell. You settle on the love of God and "suspend" His wrath because you are already convinced about His love through Christ. But for me, Greg, the love and wrath are on the same level. One calls into question the reality of the other.

So I need to kick around this hell business a little more. If I can make some sense out of this, I feel like I will have gone a long way toward making Christianity more plausible to me.

Your last letter put my mind a bit more at ease about who is going to hell, but it didn't address the problem of hell itself. This is really the more fundamental question. The Bible paints a truly nightmarish portrait of this place, does it not? It's the place of fire, hot sulfur, brimstone, darkness, torment — and the thing supposedly goes on for all eternity! Now tell me, what the hell (excuse the pun) would be the purpose of torturing someone eternally? What's the point? Obviously there's no "lesson" to be learned. This isn't *corrective* punishment. The person in hell has no hope of ever improving his character or situation. So this is sheer vengeance, pure retribution, unadulterated anger, with no motive other than the pure divine delight of inflicting horrifying pain on a person!

Don't get me wrong, Greg. There are plenty of people whom I wouldn't mind seeing in hell — *for a time.* But even *I'd* get tired of hearing Hitler scream after a couple of hundred years. Wouldn't the "fun" wear off? After that, I'd probably figure he's paid his debt to his victims, and then I'd just kill him. Why doesn't God do that? After a few hundred years He'd have already made His point. So why go on with the pain? Why not just put the sinners out of their misery? Why torture just for the sake of torture — and do so eternally?

Related to this is another point. I don't see how heaven can go on as heaven while hell is burning down below. Wouldn't the knowledge that there are billions of people boiling in hot lava down below you throughout eternity kind of dampen the "party spirit"? It seems as if this would present a problem, especially for an all-loving God who is supposedly in love with all these poor tortured souls. That must eat God up alive! Think what you'd feel like if one of your kids didn't "make it."

So it just doesn't make sense to me, Greg. And I'm just not at the point where I can pretend to "suspend" judgment about this. The character of God is on trial in my life, and this is very relevant evidence which needs to be considered.

Sincerely yours,

Dad

May 28, 1991

Dear Dad:

You said it about as forcefully as it can be said. Hell is a real theological problem, I must admit it! To be perfectly honest, Dad, I've never been able to make much sense of it myself. But I have enough grounds for believing in Jesus and in the Bible to accept what they say on this matter, even though it doesn't make perfect sense to me. If I decided to reverse this procedure and to thus reject these two authorities because their teaching on hell didn't seem reasonable to me, I'd have to then explain away all the evidences these two authorities have on their behalf. And this, I think, is harder than hell (excuse my pun) to do.

So, I believe even when I don't understand. Still, I'm not at a total loss of what to say in response to your inquiry. I am, after all, a Boyd! Let me make four general comments.

First, hardly anyone takes all the talk about hell being a place of fire and brimstone literally. The Bible uses a host of metaphors to describe this place, metaphors which would contradict each other if taken literally. So, for example, hell's described as a place of total "darkness," but also of "fire." It is described as a "pit" but also as a "lake burning with brimstone." It is described as a place of punishment, but also of total destruction. Sometimes the inhabitants are portrayed as being "cast out" from a dinner (in heaven); sometimes "cast down" into a pit; sometimes whipped by a servant. Sometimes they seem rebellious ("gnashing of teeth"), sometimes even sorrowful (Luke 16).

The metaphors, you see, vary greatly, and none of them are to be taken as a literal "snapshot" of what hell is going to be like. Rather, the goal of each is to impress on us that hell is a very bad place! *Hell is everything which is opposite of what God wants for humanity. In fact, the term* hell *itself metaphorically expresses this. Hell in Greek is* gehenna, *and gehenna was a valley outside of Jerusalem which was used as the city's major dump. What ends up in hell, the biblical authors are saying, is simply the refuse of humanity. It is the dumping grounds of the cosmos. It is the ultimate destiny of people who freely choose to live a life God never intended for them. They become "garbage." They are "cast out." They are "burned in the fire." All the metaphors in Scripture point in this direction.*

A second point, Dad, is that it is people who put themselves in hell, not God. *"God is not willing that any should perish, but that all should come to repentance,"* the Bible says. If anyone goes to hell, then, this is against God's will! It is simply inaccurate to construe God as taking any delight in people's pain. He tells us explicitly, "I take no delight in the destruction of the wicked" (Ezek. 18:23). It is, rather, the rebellious people themselves who "loved darkness instead of light" (John 3:19). Hell is where they want to be, not where God wants them to be.

Now God, to be sure, allows these people to go to hell. But He does it by giving such people their own way. Read Romans 1:20-32 carefully, Dad. Here Paul says three times about the reprobate Romans that "God gave them over to do what they wanted to do." God's judgment was giving the sinners their own way. When a person's heart is beyond hope — remember, we become the decisions that we make — God finally leaves him alone. "Go your own way," He says. And in saying this, He casts them into hell. God allows them to become eternalized in their self-creation.

This state is actually what the reprobate love, though it is nightmarishly repulsive from the perspective of those who have been touched by God's love, those who "hunger and thirst after righteousness." The alcoholic who loves his bottle above his wife, kids, and home has what he wants when they finally "leave him alone." But don't the rest of us, who are not that sick, see this as hell? Indicative of just how low this man has sunk is the fact that he thinks he is happier with his bottle than without it and with anything else. So he chooses to drink. But in truth, he is miserable. The drunk gets what he wants, but is in hell with this "privilege." He is tormented, but it is a torment of his own choosing.

So it is with God, Dad. God gives the self-addicted sinner who will not accept Him what he wants. But because of this, the sinner misses out on what life was really all about. Having cut himself off from the only lifeline of love, joy, and peace which humanity has, the individual gradually sinks into a wholly loveless, joyless, peaceless existence. It is, as C.S. Lewis once said, a sort of existence which is less than existence. He becomes refuse, not suited for the purpose God intended for him. He is now the opposite of everything God intended him to be. His existence is a tragic abortion.

A third point is this: if hell is, in fact, eternally locked (and I believe it is), then it is so "from the inside" (C.S. Lewis again). Again, it is not the will of God which keeps sinners in hell, but the will of sinners. This, *after all, is again what they* want. *The eternality of hell, then, is the eternality of a will irrationally curved in on itself, blocking out everything that would ever lead it into anything like a healthy state of being.*

Seen in this light, Dad, I don't see that there's anything all that implausible about the notion of an eternal hell. Indeed, I would maintain that only this doctrine fits our experience of human nature. As I maintained some time ago in a letter to you, is it not the case that the longer we proceed down a path, the harder it is for us ever to get off that path? Is it not the case that every moment of our lives we solidify ourselves into a certain kind of being? Are we not even now in the process of eternalizing ourselves? The biblical doctrine that there is coming a state of being where people will be permanently solidified in their respective characters is, I would think, just what an analysis of human nature would lead us to anticipate. There comes a time when no more decisions and alterations are made: this is the point where heaven and hell become eternal.

So it's simply not the case that God tortures people eternally out of some sadistic delight in inflicting pain. What pain the damned experience they inflict on themselves. And the eternality of their state is, again, completely to their own credit and preference.

A fourth and final point, Dad, is this: you wondered why God would not, after a time, finally put the rebellious out of their misery. Why doesn't He just perform a divine act of euthanasia and exterminate the damned? You should know that a number of very reputable evangelical theologians maintain that this is exactly what the Bible teaches! They maintain, on the basis of an analysis of the scriptural text, that the Bible itself teaches that God will ultimately annihilate all who are not "in Christ." The punishment is "eternal" because it has eternal effects, not because it is endured eternally. Such theologians point out that only such a view of hell squares with all the biblical talk about the reprobate "perishing," "being destroyed," "burned up like chaff," etc. The wicked "shall be as a dream when one awakens," and "they shall be as though they had not been" (Ps. 73:20; Obad. 16).

In this view, then, God's judgment and mercy converge on the same act. God judges the rebellious even as He mercifully puts them out of existence — precisely so they won't have to endure what the traditional view of hell says they endure.

While I find this view most compelling on a strictly rational level, I have some exegetical reservations with it. But I felt you should know that if you did come to believe this position, this would not place you outside of a Bible-believing faith. It is, I think, a viable option.

If this "annihilationist" position is accepted, there obviously is no problem with your worry about the coexistence of hell ruining the "party" of heaven. If it's not accepted, the problem remains, but I don't think it's insuperable.

There are a number of different ways of conceiving of the situation such that the hopelessness of hell is not a noticeable blemish on heaven. C.S. Lewis and others, for example, have speculated that the dimensions of heaven and hell may correspond to the spiritual dispositions of the inhabitants of each. Love is open, broad, expansive, inclusive, whereas selfishness is curved inward, petty, narrow, and small. From the perspective of those in hell, their reality is all there is. From the perspective of the inhabitants of heaven, however, the existence of hell is too small and too petty to notice. Hence they are "like a dream when one awakens." Isn't this pretty much the kind of relationship which petty people have with "real" people today?

Well, I doubt that I've taken away all the difficulties surrounding this doctrine, but hopefully it's a bit more plausible to you. The most important thing about hell, Dad, is not in understanding it or explaining it: it's to avoid it! Whatever theory one holds about it, it is a nightmarish reality humans were never supposed to have a part in. And yet, our race is presently so fallen, so utterly screwed up, that the only way to avoid being "disposed of" in this place is to grasp onto the Savior. He is our only hope, Dad.

Think of it this way: if Jesus willingly died for us to avoid it, hell must be one terrifying experience! The extremity of the cure shows the direness of the sickness.

With all my hope and prayers,

Greg

Isn't the Christian life impossible to live?

June 22, 1991

Dear Greg:

I've recently been reviewing our letters back and forth over the last two years, Greg, and I must say we have really come a long way! At least *I've* really come a long way! I still wake up some mornings and can't believe that I'm seriously considering all of this. But when I sit down and lay it all out before me, I *have* to seriously consider it all. I still have a good many questions and reservations and the like. But I can honestly say that it's all starting to "ring true." I'm beginning to think I'm largely over the hump on this whole thing. I never thought I'd be saying that. Thanks for your persistence, son.

Your response on hell really helped. That was a major obstacle for me. I especially liked that "annihilationist" view you mentioned. I don't know enough about the Bible to share your exegetical reservations about it, but it certainly has a lot going for it on the basis of common sense. I've always believed euthanasia was the loving thing to do in some cases, and never would this seem more obvious than when you're dealing with a person who, if you *don't* kill them, will be in pain *for all eternity!* It seems to be the only loving and just alternative. Letting someone go on, even in your revised view, strikes me as sadistic. No, it's got to be total termination. *That* kind of hell I *can* believe in.

So much for that. I'd now like to shift gears somewhat. The questions I've been finding myself asking lately, Greg, aren't as much philosophical as they are practical. If I'm thinking, about becoming a Christian, I need to know just what I'm getting into.

So here's my problem: how can God really expect anyone to live up to His ideals? I mean, I consider myself to be a pretty good person. I've certainly gone out of my way to help the underdog more than most. But I also know that my life isn't the "saintly" life the Bible idealizes. Nor could it ever be. But this biblical ideal seems to me to be totally impractical and unrealistic.

So, for example, didn't Saint Paul say somewhere that if you think about lust it's the same as doing it? Come on! One bad thought and you're an adulterer! Who could possibly live up to this? A lot of Christians say they do, but I don't believe them.

The Bible seems to have all sorts of other hang-ups on sex. Why did God slay a person for masturbating? Isn't that a wee bit extreme? And why does God give us all these sexual drives and make sex so enjoyable, only to then clamp down on us so hard with all His rules? And what of Jesus' statement that people who get remarried are committing adultery—which is why I had to get my previous marriage annulled so Jeanne could stay in the Catholic Church. It all seems quite impractical and unrealistic.

But it's not only the rigidity of the Bible's sexual ethics which bothers me. I remember hearing a priest preach on Jesus' command to "love your enemies," and I thought to myself that this command would be the ruin of any nation that actually tried to live it! So too Jesus said somewhere that if someone steals your coat you should offer him your shirt as well, or if someone hits you on one side of the face you should offer him the other side to hit as well! Come on! I bet there's not a Christian in the state of Florida who would actually do that!

So there's part of me, Greg, which says that Christianity is true and that I should believe it. But there's also part of me which says don't bother, because you could never live it anyway. And I'd rather be a sinner with integrity than a hypocritical "saint." (Which, incidentally, is why I can't ever see myself stepping inside of a church, even if I *do* become a Christian!)

Help me out if you can. I'm open to it.

With all my love and appreciation,

Dad

July 2, 1991

Dear Dad:

I can't tell you how excited I am that you are beginning to embrace the Christian faith. Always remember, Dad, it's not first and foremost a matter of what you believe. It's first and foremost a matter of whom you trust. We've needed to discuss a wide range of issues over the last two years to clear the way for this to happen. But a saving relationship with God is not forged by resolving particular issues, but by embracing the Savior as your own. Confess your need for Him. Receive His sacrifice for you. Commit your life to Him. That is it, Dad. That is everything. Everything else Christianity is about flows from this one act and is really just a footnote to it.

Now about your last letter: Dad, you are perfectly correct! No one can live the Christian life! No one has, does, or ever will (this side of heaven) perfectly live the Christian life! Do you think for a moment that I'm any better at doing the "holiness routine" than you? You know me better than that! It's as impossible for me as it is for you.

But this is just the point, Dad. It is the central motive for all of Jesus' ethical teachings. We are unable to perform our way to God on our own: thus, we need a Savior! Throughout Jesus' ministry He was confronting people who (like the Christians you've confronted) believed that they were righteous before God on the basis of how good they were. They didn't think they needed a Savior.

So how did Jesus help them? He helped them by showing them what they'd really have to be like if they were to be righteous before God without a Savior. So, for example, the Pharisees were proud because they didn't appear as sinful as other people, but Jesus tells them they need to "be perfect, even as God is perfect" (Matt. 5:48). Good luck! So too, some self-righteous folks were proud for never committing adultery, but Jesus (not Paul) told them "if you've lusted after a woman in your heart you've already committed adultery" (Matt. 5:27-28, my paraphrase). He makes His point precisely because everyone has lusted in his heart! Then again, these religious types were very proud because they had never murdered, so Jesus told them "if you get angry or even say 'fool' in your heart towards a brother, you're already in danger of hell fire" (Matt. 5:21-22, my paraphrase). The point, Dad, is that left on our own, we are all "in danger of hell fire."

The list of verses could go on, but the point would always be the same. If you're going to stand before God on your own basis, Dad, you have to be perfect, for God is perfect. Any imperfection is eternally incompatible with the character of God. Being "relatively good" just doesn't cut it. Being "sort of holy" will get no more brownie points in heaven than being a dope-addicted prostitute. One must have God's own perfect righteousness—or one has no righteousness at all that "counts."

But this righteousness, Dad, we cannot acquire through our own effort. This is the realization Jesus is driving us to with His teaching. Being rightly related to God isn't about "doing" anything. It's not a performance. If it were, as some try to make it, we'd all be goners. Rather, God's righteousness can only be received as a gift. God wants to give it to you, for free, no strings attached! He wants to establish a relationship with you, Dad, a relationship which is characterized by unconditional love. All you have to do is admit that you can do nothing, and you do this by simply accepting His righteousness. The Bible tells us the most fundamental purpose of the "law" was to bring us precisely to this point (Gal. 3).

So, Dad, hear the impossible ethics of the Sermon on the Mount, throw your hands up in the air, and confess, "I cannot do it! I quit! I am a hopeless sinner!" Read such teachings of Scripture, and recognize how badly you, like everyone else, need a Savior. And then simply accept Him. He died on the cross for your sins, Dad, so that sin no longer needs to be the issue between you and God. The only issue is, do you accept this sacrifice?

Let me close by addressing three other items raised in your letter. First, there's no record in the Bible of God ever slaying anyone for masturbating. No wonder Catholic kids grow up looking over their shoulder for thunder! I remember hearing from a nun in third grade that masturbation causes brain damage. I wasn't even sure what masturbation was, but I was certainly convinced I would never do it!

Well, none of that is in the Bible. The Bible doesn't have one thing to say about masturbation. The instance you're probably thinking of has to do with Onan who was struck dead for "spilling his seed on the ground." As strange as the passage is, however, it has nothing to do with masturbation. Onan was refusing to carry out his obligation to bear children with his brother's wife, which, from God's perspective, was a very important thing to do at the time (Gen. 38:9). In any case, it was birth control in disobedience to God that was the problem, not the wasted semen.

Secondly, concerning the political applicability of Jesus' ethics, you're right that a nation would come to disaster if it tried to survive with a "turn the other cheek" mentality. If Roosevelt and Churchill had thought this way, we'd all be Nazis now. But I hope it's clear from what I've already said about this that the main purpose of Jesus' ethics wasn't to set up a new, more restrictive, social program in this fallen world. He wasn't advocating stoning for everyone who thought about adultery; He wasn't now saying that the Old Testament allowance of divorce was no longer open; and He wasn't saying that governments should now turn the other cheek.

What He was doing was revealing how sinful our situation is. He lifts up God's ideal to drive us to the cross. But having done this, the primary function of His idealistic teaching is over. So you are right, Dad, in saying that the biblical ideals are not very practical. In a world as screwed up as ours, most practical options are to some extent sinful. And there's no way around this.

Let me close with a third and final point. I'm guessing, Dad, that you are concerned that accepting Christ is going to entail "giving up" certain things in your life. And you're not sure you can, or want, to do this. I'm guessing that you have something like the common notion that being a Christian means doing a lot of things you'd rather not do and not doing a lot of things you'd rather do.

Let me just say, Dad, that nothing could be further from the truth. You, like me, are a sinner precisely because you don't do what you need to do, and you do do what you need not do, and you like it that way. Did you follow that? And that's why you need a Savior. If you could clean up your act on your own, or even wanted to clean up your act on your own, you wouldn't need anything more than a gentle "divine encouragement" now and then. But instead, you need a Savior who suffered and died a hellish death and who is willing and able to do the whole thing for you!

So, Dad, becoming a Christian just means confessing that you need Him — precisely because you are helpless to make yourself right with God or change your own life. Being a Christian isn't about doing what you don't want to do; it's about allowing Christ to change what you want to do. Just let Him in, Dad. Let Him love you as you are. He doesn't stand far off until you make yourself clean. He wraps His arms around you and cleans you up from the inside — precisely by loving you just as you are.

The Christian life is impossible to live, Dad. Join me in it!

With love and hope,

Greg

How can another man's death pardon me?

August 14, 1991

Dear Greg:

Sorry I've been a bit slow in responding to your letters lately. Believe me, it doesn't reflect a declining interest in our discussion. In fact, it rather reflects the amount of thought I'm needing to put into each of your letters. Your last letter was pretty mind-boggling. The idea that the "rules" are there to drive us to accept salvation as a gift — that's one hell of a revolutionary concept! I've never heard of such a thing! On one level it sounds like someone trying to make a virtue out of a vice. It sounds like someone saying, "Well, since I can't live up to these high standards, I'll simply say that the purpose of the standards is to reveal the fact that I can't live up to them." But on another level your interpretation of Jesus' teachings is very compelling to me. It has the value of making sense out of something I've always known to be true: there's simply no way *anyone* can consistently live up to the ideals of Christ. Those who say they do are either blatant hypocrites or are kidding themselves.

So, as far as I'm concerned, if your interpretation is in fact making a virtue out of a vice, then we're all (Christians included!) going to hell anyway! If you're not right, being right doesn't matter at all.

But I've got another serious question I need answered, Greg. Throughout our correspondence you have continually said something to the effect of, "Jesus died for your sin." Your message seems to be that Jesus was punished for what I did, and that by believing on Him I can be all right with God. I've heard this before, but have never understood it. I just don't see how this can be. How can one man's death 2,000 years ago pardon me? How can a God of perfect justice punish Jesus for my sins, and then let me off the hook knowing full well that I'm still guilty as hell (literally)? And why would He go through all the trouble? Surely there must have been an easier way.

As always, I look forward to your response.

Love always,

Dad

August 16, 1991

Dear Dad:

I'm glad you're giving our recent dialogues so much thought. There's no hurry, so take all the time you wish in digesting each letter. I trust all is going well with you and Jeanne as of late. Has Jeanne found any new employment yet?

I really liked what you said in your last letter about the ideals of Jesus' teachings — if these aren't intended to drive us to rely completely on grace, we're all lost causes! That's it in a nutshell, Dad. One advantage that obviously worldly people like you and I have over the "well-bred religious people" is that we tend to get this central point of Jesus' teachings more easily than the religious folk. We know we have no alternative! *People like the Pharisees who keep a pretty nice polished image of themselves are much more apt to think that they're pretty holy on their own and thus are capable of* earning *God's acceptance by a good performance. So they're more inclined to hear Jesus' teachings as a challenge for their self-righteous effort. The more difficult the teaching, the more strenuous their effort. So when they hear Jesus say "be as perfect as God," they don't crumble up and cry out for mercy: they desperately strive to actually do this! And for them, salvation hangs on this.*

173

This is not only a serious misunderstanding of Jesus' teachings, it is also extremely destructive. If one really believes that his salvation hangs on his own goodness, he can only live with himself by convincing himself that he is in fact "perfect enough" for God. But since everyone is sinful, in their heart and mind if not also in their behavior, this perfectionism entails that such religious people must become experts at living in self-deception. *They must, as you said, constantly "kid themselves." They must systematically suppress every introspective thought which might tell them that they are failing to meet Jesus' "challenge." This is why legalistic religious people are usually very shallow — the leaders more so than the others because they are the ones who have "proven themselves" to be "successful" at this self-deceptive game. Everything that doesn't fit the religious image these people want so hard to maintain must simply be "shoved in the closet." It must go below the surface of their consciousness.*

This is simply sick. It means that every problem that needs addressing in these peoples' lives, and every wound that needs healing, can never be addressed or healed. All emotional and spiritual sickness is treated like an indictment and is therefore covered over by religious pretense. And the consequences of this are obviously very destructive. Every neurosis, Scott Peck says, is the result of refusing to confront the truth. You can temporarily cover over reality with a polished appearance, but reality, in the end, always wins. This is why legalistic individuals and churches are frequently so dysfunctional. They stuff everything which needs to be exposed. What happened with Jimmy Swaggart is, I suspect, a classic case-in-point.

In any case, I think it is perfectly clear that the central thrust of Jesus' teaching was to do just the opposite *of what legalism does. Rather than inspire giant feats of self-effort which result in denying the sinful reality of our inner life, Jesus was trying to bring about the end of all self-effort by getting us to examine the sinful reality of our inner lives. And it works, if one hears Him rightly.*

When one hears the impossibility *of Jesus' ideals, when one finally gives up on his own self-effort as a means of impressing God, when one finally realizes that all he is and ever shall be before God is due to God's performance, not his, then one is free to be real with what is going on in one's life. One is free to be open and honest about all his faults, shortcomings, sin, etc. One can see that nothing hangs on pretending he's something he's not. As a friend of mine (Jeff Van-Vondren) says a lot, "Only when how things look is irrelevant can how things are be addressed and changed." And this, every psychologist will tell you, is the central ingredient to all mental and emotional (and spiritual) health!*

So in a word, the Cross of Christ and grace of God mean it's safe before God to be real, honest, and therefore healthy. How relatively "good" or "bad" a person is is completely beside the point. Grace is, as you said so eloquently, Dad, "one hell of a revolutionary concept."

Well, sorry for getting "preachy," but I see this insight as being both the most central, and the most misunderstood, tenet of Christianity. But let me move on now to your question about how Christ's death brings about your pardon.

To be perfectly up front with you, Dad, I really don't know how this occurs. The church has never arrived at any definitive theology of how we are made right with God through the work of the cross (what's called "the atonement"). I don't think we should be too surprised at this, however. If we find the fundamental structure of physical reality to be impervious to our reason — science is increasingly arriving at just this conclusion — should we find it surprising if the central act whereby God redeems the world is also clouded in mystery? I think not. Nevertheless, there are two things which I'd like to say which might clear up the matter for you somewhat.

First, Dad, it's important to realize that Jesus was not just "a man" whose death 2,000 years ago gets you off the hook. Jesus was not an innocent "third party" that God punished in place of us. Rather, Jesus is Himself God as well as man. He is not only the one judged for the crime; He is the One against whom the crime is committed, and the One who passes out the sentence for the crime. The Judge Himself became the judged! So there is no "third party" in this transaction, Dad. There are only two parties — the all-holy God and sinful humanity — and the Jesus who died for us is both. This is not injustice, Dad; this is incomprehensible love.

175

Secondly, without trying to explain exactly how *the atonement oc-curred, or whether it* had *to happen the way it did, I think we are given enough insight in Scripture to make sense of the fact* that *it occurred the way it did. We can say* why *Jesus died for us without going so far as to say that He* had *to die for us.*

Three considerations, I believe, will help us make sense of Jesus' death for us. First, God is an all-holy God. Sin is thus fundamentally incompatible with Him. It is contrary to His nature, like arsenic is to ours. What is more, since God is perfect, He must be self-consistent. If God were ever inconsistent with His own character, He could only be so in the direction of imperfection. Thus, God is perfectly opposed to sin, and is perfectly consistent and unqualified in this opposition.

But, secondly, holiness isn't God's only attribute; God is also perfectly loving. "God is love" the Bible says. He created creatures other than Himself out of this love, and He has continued to be passionately in love with us even though we have universally fallen into sin. In spite of our sin, God wants us to live eternally with Him.

This raises a dire problem, however, and this is my third consideration. The problem is, how can created beings who are hopelessly sinful be rendered compatible with an all-holy God who is necessarily opposed to all sin? I would argue that two things need to happen.

1. *Our sin must be "atoned for." It cannot simply be overlooked. (Our inclination to sometimes overlook sin is due to our imperfect moral character, yet even we usually feel wronged when serious crimes go unpunished. Justice must be served!)*

2. *We must be* changed *into beings who are compatible with God, and who, therefore, are perfect. If either of these things is left undone, our eternal lives must be spent as arsenic in God's stomach!*

So the million dollar question becomes, how are these two things going to occur? The biblical teaching is that they could never occur on humanity's own effort. Our situation in sin is far too severe for this. Left to ourselves we do not even want to "pay" for our own sins, and even if we did want to, we'd have to die (eternally) to do it! What is more, our situation in sin is such that we don't on our own want to change ourselves, and even if we did want to change ourselves, we couldn't do it. Our enslavement to sin prevents us from desiring, and certainly from achieving, perfection in holiness.

So if the two things are going to be accomplished, they must be accomplished by God Himself, not us. And this, Dad, is exactly what the Bible says happened in the life and death of Jesus Christ. In Jesus, God's love absorbed His own justice. Out of love for humanity, God Himself satisfied His own moral standard by absorbing within Himself the sin of humanity and the punishment which that sin deserved. As a man, God "became sin, that we might be made the righteousness of God" (2 Cor. 5:19). In Jesus, humanity pays for its sin, and God justly judges that sin, for Jesus is both God and man. Hence sin is atoned for and is no longer an issue between God and man. Christ thus accomplishes the first necessary condition in making us eternally compatible with God.

Christ also accomplishes the second necessary condition for humanity to be compatible with God as well — we are eternally changed! The Bible says that when a person accepts what God has done for him in Christ, God gives him His own perfect righteousness, *the only kind of righteousness which is compatible with God. In the Book of Romans, Paul says,* "To the man who does not work (try to earn God's love by his behavior) but who simply trusts God who justifies the wicked, his faith is credited as righteousness" (4:5). *When you trust in Christ as your only hope of salvation, Dad, God not only forgives you all past, present, and future sin (condition 1), but He also gives you His own perfect righteousness (condition 2). And He can consistently do the latter because He has done the former. You are given a new godlike nature.* "We are new creatures in Christ Jesus," *the Bible says.* "Old things have passed away, behold all things are new" (2 Cor. 5:17).

This does not, obviously, mean that people are perfect from the moment they give their lives to the Lord. A believer is given a "new self," a self identified with the righteousness of God. But he yet lives under a habitual addiction to the thoughts, emotions, and behaviors of "the old self," the self which is identified with everything other than God. Believers are thus given a new nature which is what they truly are, but they yet live, in varying degrees, in contradiction to this new nature. Only in heaven will the gift of God's eternal righteousness shine forth from us perfectly. Only then will the "old self" be shown to be the lie that it is. Our time on earth after our conversion is simply a slow progression toward this end.

Now a lot more could be said about the work of Christ if I had the time to go into it. While making us compatible with the Father was, I think, a central motive behind the work of the Cross, there are other motives as well. Scripture, for example, makes it clear that Jesus' death on the cross somehow dealt a death blow to Satan and his demonic forces which have had the world under siege since our fall. (See Col. 2:14ff, and Heb. 2:14.) It is also clear that Jesus came to instruct us, to make God visible to us, to give us a perfect human example to aspire toward, as well as to accomplish several other things. It seems to fit the wisdom of God to kill a number of flies with one swat. But we can't go into these other motives now.

Well, I hope what I have said has been helpful, Dad. Let me add one final word. The work of Christ is like a billion dollar bank account which God has individually laid aside for all His children to freely inherit. And He wants everyone to be one of His children. But it all just sits there, utterly worthless, until you personally claim your birthright, Dad. You must accept this inheritance. God's beautiful plan of salvation comes to nothing if a person doesn't accept it as his own. But when one inherits it, one inherits the whole thing! Though you are a sinner, you instantly stand before the Father with the righteousness of Jesus Christ when you believe. Not one spot does He find on you! "As far as the east is from the west," the Bible says, "so far has God removed our transgressions from us" (Ps. 103:12). You can face your Creator, who is also your Savior, with joy, not fear.

My prayer for you, Dad, is that understanding will turn to action, and you will take all of this to be true for you. Inherit the kingdom!

With all my love and hope,

Greg

How can I be holy and sinful at the same time?

September 12, 1991

Dear Greg:

Thanks for your little treatise on why Jesus died. It's very informative and sheds some light on something which has been puzzling to me for some time.

Your understanding of God's grace is so strange, Greg, that I almost think it *must* be a revelation from the Almighty because I can't imagine a person ever dreaming up such a counterintuitive notion! Common sense says that people go to heaven or hell depending on whether they're good or bad, and this is what I always thought Christians believe. But you're saying that this isn't even close to being true. Do I really understand you correctly? You're in or out depending on your belief in Christ. Absolutely revolutionary!

I'm not yet in the position where I want to turn "understanding into action," as you say. But I suspect it's just a matter of time. When I make this commitment, I know it has to be genuine. And I just don't feel it's time yet.

In the meantime, I have another question about this salvation business. It's basically this: I don't get how I can be totally holy before God, even though everyone else who knows me knows I'm not holy. Is God blind or something? Maybe I'm misunderstanding you. You say that our sin must be *forgiven* and that we must be *changed* if we're to have a relationship with God. Well, I can see how God forgives our past sins because of Jesus, but I don't see that Christians are changed *in the present*. How are Christians perfectly compatible with God in the present when they aren't yet perfectly changed? If one sin separates us from God, having all my past sins forgiven won't do me much good because I'll sure as hell blow it every day. So, Greg, tell me how I can be holy and sinful at the same time?

With all my love,

Dad

October 3, 1991

Dear Dad:

I loved the question of your last letter. I don't know if you noticed it or not, but our letters are sort of "changing gear." We really aren't arguing whether Christianity is true (apologetics) anymore. We're rather now discussing how Christianity is true (theology). Your questions seem to come much more from the perspective of one inside the faith. This is really exciting to me. It s just "a matter of time" as you say, but I've always believed this!

So, how can we be holy and sinful at the same time? I'll explain it with this analogy. When God created the world in the beginning, He said, "Let there be light" and there was light. He said, "Let there be dry ground," and there was dry ground. And so on. God's Word, we see, creates the reality it speaks. To use philosophical terminology, God's word is "ontologically productive." It creates being.

Now our salvation is no less the result of God's word than is our creation. God says, "All the sin of Ed Boyd's past is gone," and all your sin is gone! And God says, "Ed Boyd is perfectly holy before Me," and you are perfectly holy before Him. God's word defines what is real and what is true. No one, and no thing, can argue with God. "If God is for us, who can be against us?" the Apostle Paul says. "It is God Himself who declares us to be righteous" (Rom. 8). So if God says you're righteous because of your faith, Dad, you are righteous!

180

But God's word of salvation differs from God's word of creation in one important respect. When God spoke His word of creation, there was nothing there to resist it. There was only nothingness. But when God speaks His word of salvation, there is something there to resist it. There is already an existing Ed Boyd, full of old ways of thinking, acting, feeling, etc., and many aspects of this "old self" are opposed to what God says about you.

Now God isn't going to just annihilate the "old" Ed Boyd and re-create a "new" Ed Boyd. If He did that, He wouldn't be saving you at all: He'd be creating an entirely different person. But it's you, in all your old sin, that God loves and wants to save. So He works to re-create you, and me, and everyone else, from the inside out. When you put your trust in the Savior, Dad, God speaks the word of your eternal righteousness, your unspotted perfection, into your life. This is now what is "most true" about you. Yet God doesn't simply bulldoze over what was already there. He simply renders it "false." It is no longer what is ultimately true about you. This is why it is called "the old self." In time the truth, the "new self," will outgrow this "old self."

So we are made new creatures in Christ the moment we believe. All of our sin is absorbed in the Cross, and all of Christ's righteousness is imputed to us. We are forgiven, *and we are* changed. *But we do not instantaneously manifest this truth in our lives. Our "old" (and now false) habitual way of thinking often doesn't accept our forgiveness. Our "old" (and now false) habitual way of living opposes the change which God effects in our heart. Our old (and now false) self-identity, defined by all previous experiences and inclinations and feelings and ambitions which we've had, simply takes time to die out. Only in heaven will what we "truly are" be manifested untarnished.*

So how are believers holy and sinful at the same time? In terms of their re-created essence, *they are holy, but in terms of how they* manifest *this essence in their thoughts, feelings, and actions, they are yet sinful. In terms of* God's *perspective of what they shall* become, *believers are holy, but in terms of* their *perspective of what they* now are, *they are sinners. In terms of what is* ultimately true, *as defined by God, they*

181

are holy, but in terms of what is ultimately false, *as defined by every other source, they are sinners. In terms of who they are* "in Christ," *they are perfectly holy, but in terms of who they are* "in themselves," *apart from Christ, they are wholly sinners. Are you getting it, Dad?*

Christians, then, are each much like a butterfly in a cocoon. The life of beauty, of flying, of gracefulness is within them — it's who they truly are — but this life is enclosed inside something which is inherently opposed to beauty, flying, and gracefulness. They are destined to fly, but in the meantime their life is a life of transition. They are butterflies in the process of shedding their cocoons.

What is, I think, very important for you to realize, Dad, is that the way in which Christians are gradually freed from their "old" selves is not by their own hard work, but by just allowing the Lord to build up and strengthen the butterfly within them. The only food which the saved soul eats is God's love, and so it is only as we rest in the love which God has for us, even while we are yet in the cocoon, that we receive more and more strength and motivation to get out of the cocoon. As we let Jesus love us as we are, we increasingly become convinced that we can bust loose, we can be freed, we can fly — and the more we want to do so.

Thus, don't imagine for a moment, Dad, that you can free yourself from your cocoon, or that you could on your own even want to be set free very badly. Your motivation and strength for living God's life only comes when God's life is already residing within you. Transformation is the effect, not the cause, of salvation.

So the one thing you do need to do, Dad, is to let God's life reside in you, and you do this by confessing that you are a sinner without hope in yourself and by accepting Jesus Christ as your Savior. Let God love you and accept you as you are, and slowly you will feel the internal desire and strength to become something different than what you are. Letting Him save you — that is the only thing you need to worry about. Why hold back any longer, Dad?

Hope this makes things a little bit clearer.

With love, hope, and anticipation,

Greg

How can I be sure it's all true?

November 11, 1991

Dear Greg:

I trust all is going well with you and the family these days. I see you've been buried in snow the last few weeks. That was some Halloween storm you had! It brings back very "unfond" memories for me. The summer heat may be bad down here, but at least I don't have to break my back shoveling myself out of it to get to the end of the driveway! In any case, I can't tell you how much Jeanne and I are looking forward to having all of you down here with us next month on your Disney World "mother of all vacations."

OK, on to our "debate" (if you can call it that anymore). Your last letter had a lot of heavy theology in it, and I'm not sure I understand it all. Your distinction between our "essence" and how we "manifest" it is a bit difficult to grasp. Or maybe the problem is that it sounds too good to be true. I don't know. In any case, I'm inclined to believe it. Unless something like your distinction is true, no one stands a chance of making it into heaven.

Here's where I find myself, Greg. I want to believe, but I find it difficult to genuinely do so. I mean, you've made a rock solid case for your belief, and you've answered all my objections and questions, but I still find myself somewhat up in the air on the whole thing, and I'm not sure why. How can you be *sure* it's all true? I keep thinking maybe there's something we've missed. Maybe there's a fallacy in your argument that I overlooked. Maybe there are some relevant facts in your historical presentation of Christ that have been omitted, or that perhaps aren't discovered yet but which will overturn your entire argument when they are discovered. Why do other very intelligent people, many of them scholars, reject your arguments and therefore reject Christianity?

So I feel I'm on the precipice of faith, but I don't yet have the confidence to take the leap. I still have doubts, but I don't know what further thing you could say to me which would alleviate these. Maybe I just need more time.

Give me your advice.

Lots of love,

Dad

November 22, 1991

Dear Dad:

I really appreciate your honesty, Dad — I have throughout our correspondence. I also have a great deal of admiration for your integrity. I wish I had more of that kind of character that resolutely refuses to act disingenuously.

To be perfectly candid, I'm not sure where to go from here in our discussion. My role as "apologist" seems to have come to an end, but maybe some pastoral advice will be in order — if you don't mind getting this from your son. Let me make several suggestions.

First, concerning the lingering intellectual doubts. I'd recommend that you peruse our past correspondence from time to time. Sometimes the force of an argument can diminish with time. One can forget why one found a particular argument convincing, and thus doubt about it arises again. This happens to me all the time on a lot of different issues. When this happens, I go back and review the issue. Sometimes I find that, as a matter of fact, something was overlooked, and the issue is reopened. Other times I just reconfirm for myself the validity of the case I originally accepted as true. In either event, it helps to go back. If you find that something was overlooked, by all means let's reopen the discussion about it.

Secondly, I'm wondering if you have a misconception about the kind of certainty faith involves, Dad. No matter what people believe, Dad, their belief will go beyond what the evidence requires them to believe. That's why it's a belief, and not certainty. This is true whether a person believes Christianity is true, or whether he believes Christianity is false. On an intellectual level, both positions involve some degree of risk. One simply cannot have the kind of certainty one has in mathematics about either position. The question is not which belief is strictly required by the evidence, but which belief has the best evidence to support it. I believe, and I think you believe, that Christianity has much more going for it as a worldview than any alternative. But neither of us commits a logical contradiction if we deny it.

So, there is always a "leap" involved in believing anything. But what I want you to see, Dad, is that you are already taking this "leap." A person who chooses not to believe, or even just to suspend judgment, is taking a tremendous risk, a tremendous "leap of faith," for he may be wrong, and this may have severe consequences for him. It's like being in a house and someone outside hollers "fire"! You can choose to believe him or not to believe him — and you weigh the evidence carefully (do you smell smoke? do you see flames? etc.). You can choose to believe and risk looking foolish for running out of your house if it's a joke, or you can choose not to believe and risk being burned up. If you choose to suspend judgment, you risk the same thing. So there simply is no "risk free" position, not even the position of not taking a position.

To switch metaphors, it seems to me that life is very much like a certain train ride. We are all on a train heading with ever increasing speed toward a cliff. We don't know when we shall run out of track, but we are certain we shall at some point run out. Some on this train say that what you believe will allow you to survive this derailment, others say not. We're all going to just die. You have an unspecified limited amount of time to decide. To decide not to decide is to decide, for one's survival hangs on what one believes — if the people who claim this are correct. So you weigh all the available evidence for each claim, you consider all the options, you consider all the risks — and the train is speeding up. The cliff nears. What will your decision be?

The most reasonable thing to do, Dad, is to believe! The evidence is strong. The alternatives are comparably weak. And the risk of not believing is far greater than the risk of believing. As Blaise Pascal said (in his famous "Pascal's Wager"), if Christianity is false, you've lost nothing. If it's true, you've lost all eternity. Christianity, therefore, is clearly the best bet!

But let me add one more thing to this. The uncertainty of faith is much greater for a person in your shoes than it is for someone in mine. For once one becomes a Christian, once one accepts Christ as his Savior and begins to cultivate a relationship with Him, the certainty of faith increases. Christ becomes a living reality. One knows Him not only (or even primarily) on the basis of the evidence, but on the basis of an experiential relationship.

So I'm imploring you, Dad, wager your life on Christ. If it seems "risky" now, it will seem far less so in time. And, after all, there is nothing to lose, and everything to gain.

I have one final bit of "pastoral" advice to share with you. I'm sure that a great deal of your reservation about Christianity has nothing to do with evidence, but is rather simply connected with the fact that this is all very new to you. It seems "unreal" because you've never thought like this before. It's a new way of seeing yourself and the world. It's a new way of living. So it's not surprising that you have reservations about it.

What will help, Dad, is if you just slowly begin to "get into" the Christian way of thinking and living. This is also part of "the wager." You start by simply laying down all your cards because it's the best bet, but you gradually grow into it as a reality.

So I'm sending you some Christian musical tapes of the sort of music I think you like. I encourage you to just listen to them when you can. This will, I think, help you "grow into" the Christian walk. As you listen, think about the lyrics. Try to picture the message they're singing about in your mind. Let the beauty of Christ come to you through the music, and you'll find yourself gradually falling in love with Christ.

I'm also sending you a Bible and some devotional reading material. These also will help you "grow into" the faith. I encourage you to start reading the Gospel of John. Read it very slowly, think about it, but don't worry at all if much of it doesn't make sense to you. Just get out of it what you can. Do the same with the devotional material. Just let it sink in as much as it can.

I also encourage you to begin attending a Bible-believing church in your area. I know how you feel about churches, so maybe this one will have to be put on the back burners for a while. But it can really help to join in worship with people who share your faith.

Finally, Dad, I encourage you to try to just talk to God now and then. This doesn't have to be a formal thing — I know you have a hang-up on this from your Catholic days. But just talk to Jesus as you'd talk to me. To the extent you are able (but don't worry about this), just close your eyes and picture Jesus, and speak to Him in a very natural way. I find that doing this with the Christian music playing softly in the background works well. This will no doubt seem strange and awkward at first, but in time you'll get used to it.

The simple prayer which begins the whole thing, Dad, the prayer which the Bible says constitutes salvation itself, goes something like this:

> Lord, I know I'm a sinner, and I'm sorry for this. I believe that You died for my sins so I could live eternally in heaven with You. So I now want to accept You as my Lord and Savior. Come into my life, Lord Jesus, and make me what You want me to be.

This is the sort of prayer all Christians pray when they become Christians. This simple prayer is what instantaneously makes a person spotless before God the Father. Nothing you'll ever do in your life will make you more perfect before God than you are the moment you pray this prayer. And when you do it, Dad, you may not feel any different, but the Bible says that all the angels in heaven and the Lord God Himself will erupt in rejoicing celebration. And you can bet that I'll be joining them!

So the question, Dad, is not really how can you risk believing in Christ. The question is, how can you risk doing otherwise? Take the jump, Dad. You'll never regret it.

I'll be in touch with you. I hope the next time I write you I won't be closing the letter "with hope," but instead "with joy."

You know how much I love you,

Sincerely with hope,

Greg

EPILOGUE

I believe

A Note by Greg Boyd

After my written reply on November 11, the correspondence between my father and I became exclusively a phone correspondence. We called each other a number of times, and I had an extended visit with him during the two months following our last written correspondence. The Christian faith was always the main (and usually only) topic of conversation. And with each conversation my father grew less hesitant about committing his life to Christ. Finally, on January 15, 1992 Edward K. Boyd "gave in" and accepted Jesus Christ as his personal Lord and Savior.

The following is part of the letter he sent me as a follow-up to his conversion experience.

January 21, 1992

Dear Greg:

Well, as I told you over the phone, I finally "took the leap." Hallelujah! As I sit here and read over all of our correspondence, I still can't believe how I've changed from a smart-ass-know-it-all to an actual believer! Jeanne can't believe it either! It's probably even confused the hell out of our dog! The angels whom you say rejoice over this sort of thing are probably giving each other high-fives! Have you told Anita yet? I'll bet she'll be floored.

Looking back on it, it seems that things really began to change for me when you convinced me of the Bible's inspiration and helped me make sense out of hell. I'm not sure why, but I think it was at that point that I really started to "see the light." Around this time

I began to get the distinct impression that my case for skepticism was ultimately a lost cause. I recall being at once confused, a bit scared, but also excited when I came to this realization. Now I'm just excited. It wouldn't have happened without your persistence, Son, and I want you to know that I love and appreciate you for this.

As you know, I've still got a number of questions, and I'm sure we'll continue to hash these out. But my disposition has completely changed. I'm asking them no longer as a skeptic, but as a believer. You don't need to end your letters "with hope" any longer.

Keep in touch and keep me in prayer. I'm reading the Bible a lot lately, and it's beginning to make a little sense. But any material you can send to help me will be appreciated. Prayer is still tough, but I have a feeling it will probably come with time. I'm not up-tight about it. I'm forgiven.

Lots of love, with faith(!)

Dad